DANGER AND PLAY

Essays on Embracing Masculinity

By Mike Cernovich

Cover design by Artful

Book formatting by MPP Freelance

Contents

Business and Career Success

Mindset

Motivation and Inspiration

Masculinity

8 TRAITS OF MASCULINE MEN

Guys regularly complain that American women aren't feminine. Yet, if you want a feminine woman, should you not first be masculine? What are some traits of masculine men and how can you use these masculine traits to attract women?

Proving that wisdom is often found in unusual sources, Planned Parenthood provides some decent guidelines for masculinity. Planned Parenthood claims these masculine traits are "socially constructed," which is silly. Masculinity is a biological construct.

Nevertheless, the list is quite good. A quick review of this list shows that most American men are not prepared to handle feminine women.

Traits Commonly Associated with Masculinity

1. **Independent**. Are you always crying about politics, saying that life will be good for everyone if "your man" is elected? Do you complain that the government has not done enough to boost the economy? Then you are dependent upon the government for your economic success.

2. **Non-emotional**. Do you cry when people say things that hurt your feelings? Have you ever reported an online message board post to a moderator because it was "mean?" When your boss is being an ass, do you become a sad little panda?

3. **Aggressive**. Are you afraid of approaching women? Do you take what is yours or complain that there is a lack of opportunity? Can you survive a street fight, or would you become a victim of the Knockout Game?

4. **Tough-skinned**. Does a rhinoceros know when a gnat is on its back? Do you stew and brew over real and perceived slights? See number two, above.

5. **Competitive**. Do you try making yourself better each day? Do you grind out extra reps in the weight room, look for a side hustle, and constantly improve?

6. **Strong, active, and self-confident**. Do you walk like a man? Are you in the gym and reading every day? Do you have the posture of an alpha male? Or do you walk with slouching shoulders and hold your head down like a slave before going home to play your Xbox? Do you live by the Twin Pillars of Alpha?

7. **Hard**. When life gets tough, do you push through or do you quit? Are you afraid of drinking a green juice and instead look for your milk and cookies? Even worse, are you so defeated and demoralized by life that you become a drunk?

8. **Sexually aggressive**. Any loser can be horny. When you see a woman, do you decide that you are going to be a man and make your move?

Life is about polarity. It's yin and yang. Feminine women want masculine men.

Women want their opposite. Even a self-proclaimed "strong, independent woman" wants to be tamed. All of my feminist classmates—including aggressive lawyers—changed their last names when getting married.

America is full of feminine women, as femininity is a biological construct. Women want to submit to a man. Or did you not notice that *50 Shades of Grey* sold over 50 million copies?

Women want masculine men. There just aren't enough masculine men to go around.

You're Not Entitled to Happiness

The two pillars of feminism are narcissism and entitlement. Because American men are feminized, American men are as unhappy as women.

Narcissism is mistakenly interpreted to mean vanity. If that were true, there would be no fat or ugly narcissists. Rather than denoting vanity, narcissism is the belief that the world exists for you and you alone and that any craving is therefore morally virtuous, deserving of immediate satisfaction. (American obesity explained in a sentence: "I'm entitled to indulge whatever craving my body feels.")

Consider the attitudes of many American men, even men who read game blogs and thus who are trying to "unplug" from mainstream thought. Men are always bitching (note that *bitching* is a feminine world; real men don't bitch) about this stuff:

- Clubs suck.
- American women suck.
- My friends suck.
- Learning game sucks.
- Life sucks.
- Spending money on dates sucks.
- Going to the gym sucks.
- New York City sucks.

If you want to understand the narcissism epidemic, add *for me* to each of those sentences. You then understand that American men are not bitching about the state of affairs *qua* the state of

affairs (none of us are that enlightened),
but instead are bitching bout the state of affairs *qua* how that
impacts me.

The truth is that while American women suck in general, there
are plenty of guys pulling hot ass. Some of us have legit friends
who have our backs when needed. Some of us are legit friends
who are there when our friends need us. Some of us have great
times in clubs: even clubs in New York.

There is more truth.

If you are out of shape, broke, have no game, have no
personality, have a negative personality, are always bitching
about how inferior everyone is to yourself (and telling everyone
how superior you are), life will suck *for you*. Everything and
everyone will suck *for you*.

Life sucks only *for you* when you feel entitled to happiness.

Most men think that by virtue of "showing up" to life, they
should be rewarded with riches and pussy; or, at the very least,
they are entitled to a decent-looking housewife who fucks them
regularly and doesn't cheat, a 9 to 5 job (weekends off, natch) that
pays enough to sustain a family, two kids, dog, and white picket
fence.

Why are you entitled to any of this?

In 1912, Americans lived with their extended families
in dilapidated homes and walked around shoeless.

In 1992, I had two pairs of jeans to last me an entire school
year. I was fat. I got bullied. My mom was mentally ill. We had
food stamps.

You'll rarely hear me bitch because when you are born with
little, you feel entitled to nothing. If I wanted to have decent
clothes, I had to get away from my hometown. If I wanted to stop
being bullied, I had to get tougher than the bullies.

Because I focused so much on beating people up, my social
skills were lacking. I didn't have any friends or girlfriends. In

response, I read over a hundred books on communication, body language, human interaction, emotional intelligence, human evolution, culture and philosophy. Now things are great.

Life is simple when you realize, "Everything that sucks is my fault. Either my emotional response to the situation is overborne or else I am not doing enough to change my external environment."

When guys bitch, all I can think is, "Why do you think the world should be any other way? Why should life be different for you? What have you done that entitles you to righteous treatment?"

Oh, that's right. You exist and therefore are endowed by your Creator with the inalienable right to endless pussy, good friends, cash money, and eternal youth.

Why do you think being born is an accomplishment? Motivated by billions of years of evolution, your dad was driven to inseminate your mom to replicate his genes. You were born. Great fucking job, kiddo. Let's all sit around and talk about how fucking special that makes you.

After we're done listening to how much life sucks, guess what: life will still suck *for you.*

If you want life to stop sucking, find out where you fucked up. Maybe you're a shitty person who deserves every bad thing that has happened to you. Maybe you're a decent person who lacks a life philosophy. Maybe you're living in the wrong town, have the wrong job, or are dating the wrong girls.

(I used to think I had clinical depression. Then I moved from a shitty flyover state to a Golden Land. Suddenly, my depression was cured. A few years later I was unhappy again. Then I got divorced and got happy.)

Accept that you are not entitled to happiness. Accept that if you want to be happy, you must figure out what makes you happy. Make changes.

Or else, join a goddamned knitting circle with a bunch of old ladies, because legit men are done listening to how much your life sucks. You'll never build a solid crew if you yourself suck.

How to Be a More Dominant Man: Part 1. Mindset

A cold wind blew through my bathroom window. As cold water rained down on my chest and I shivered and hacked and pissed down the drain, all I could think about was how a towel fresh from the dryer would feel. Feeling weakness overtaking my body, I shifted my mindset and engaged in state-changing self-talk:

"You are done when I say we are done."

If you are wondering what a story about a contrast shower has to do with dominating other men and women, good. You're likely confused because your thinking about domination—like mine was until recently—is backwards.

We all think about domination from the wrong direction. We think about dominating others when we should first think about dominating ourselves. How can you dominate others when you can't exercise the force of will needed to dominate yourself?

Think about domination from the inside-out rather than the outside-in by taking on a common complaint: "These American women are just so gosh darn awful. I can't keep them from mistreating me!" Do you know who is worse than the most entitled woman? You!

Who gives you more drama on any given day: some random girl or the entitled princess of your body?

- "I don't want to get out of bed. Let's cuddle with the blanky."
- "I don't want to edit my blog posts."

- I will not change my state. My emotions rule me. I want to BLINDLY RAGE AND "SCREAM!!!"
- "I want to get fuuuuuuuuuuuuuuuuuuuccccccked up."
- "I want to watch porn."
- "High Intensity Training burns. Stop the set!"

Want, don't want, whine, bitch, piss, moan. We're a bunch of six-year olds trapped in mens' bodies. Most of the time we give in to these transient feelings. We lack the resolve to say:

"No. We are done when I say we are done."

Does your girl mistreat you because she is the Big Bad Wolf or because your weakness reverberates through your soul? Do your co-workers walk all over you because they are evil or because they can sense that you are weak? Are *they* the problem or are *you* the problem?

"People can only get away with what you let them get away with."

Why should people treat you as anything other than a weakling and a pushover when your every action indicates that's exactly what you are?

Are you being *mis*treated or treated exactly like you deserve to be treated?

An alpha male learns to dominate his body before he worries about what everyone else is doing. He builds discipline.

Once you can dominate yourself, dominating others comes far more naturally. You get used to dealing with the most pathetic, needy, nasty (and beautiful, godlike, and blessed) invention ever created: your human body.

As you dominate yourself, something cool happens. You develop a sense of quietude, an Alpha Zen attitude towards life. This vibe or aura begins to radiate from your soul. You become unshakeable.

Blind rage turns into focused anger turns into an intensity that burns and destroys all who would dare to challenge you.

Others learn not to mess with you unless they are hiding behind a keyboard.

You are unshakeable, because how can the outside world shake your mind when that pathetic weak body of yours remains under your iron grip?

Do not learn how to master others until you have first mastered yourself.

(Learn how to master your mindset.)

How to Become a More Dominant Man: Part 2. Body Language and Physical Presence

Two types of social dominance.

Social dominance can be understood in one of two ways: dominating others or not being dominated. I tend to think of dominance as the latter; that is, to be able to do my own thing.

If you want to become a CEO, then read your *48 Laws of Power*. I am not particularly interested in dominating others in the *48 Laws of Power* understanding of the term, because leadership is slavery.

Let's say I wanted to increase the audience for *Danger & Play*. I could build a huge audience if I changed my tone and changed topics. I could tell normal people they are great instead of telling them to go away.

It would come at a great personal cost to my soul. I would have to water down my message. I would be a slave to whiners and complainers, asking before publishing each post, "What if I offend someone?" I'd need to be politically correct and I'd need to tolerate the weakness that exists in the majority of today's men.

I most certainly will not.

Danger & Play is my soul and I will never pollute it to become a leader of pathetic hanger-ons and other space-taker-uppers.

I seek to be dominant in the sense that other people leave me alone and let me go about my business in peace. When I'm in groups, my wishes are respected and criminals know better than to mess with me.

There is substantial overlap, however, and if you can go without being dominated, then chances are you will find that you are often the leader of the group. Even a longer can develop charisma.

Rule 1. Eye contact *uber alles* (and put your damned iPhone in your pocket unless you want to look like a victim).

Respect the power of eye contact. If you have solid eye contact game, you have met the 80/20 rule. Eighty percent of your success with other people will be met by taking the 20% move of making and holding eye contact.

If you have poor eye contact, nothing else on this list matters. Eyes are the gateway to the soul. If you look down at the ground like a servant, you have revealed yourself as a slave who does not look up at his master. It also makes you look like a victim.

The other day, a fine urban youth living in Section 8 housing was standing in the middle of the street. I saw a girl on the corner, another fine lady, and could sense what was about to transpire.

This fine fellow started to move diagonally towards me. I looked him in the eyes and smirked. With a look I communicated that I welcomed his affections.

He stopped, looked down, and shuffled his feet back to where he was standing.

Had I looked down at the ground, I may have ended up like poor little Matt Yglesias, a self-hating liberal who was a victim of the Knockout Game.

The truth is that I wish he had come closer. I would have thrown a brutal overhand right once he was within distance and reminded him that not all men of my socioeconomic status walk the streets in fear.

When you meet someone, look them in the eyes. Hold your gaze for 1-3 seconds, long enough to register that you've looked them in the eyes but not long enough to look like a creep.

Exception: There's one notable exception to eye contact and the streets.

If some really criminal type looks you in the eye mean mugging you and it looks like you might have to get into a fight, you should still not look down. Instead, keep your chin up and look the side. This allows the goon to save face (you're not directly challenging him by holding eye contact) while also suggesting to him that he seek out a weaker target (since you did not look down showing him you're weak and thus someone to victimize).

That's how you diffuse a potentially hostile situation without punking out. He saves face. You save face and don't look like a victim.

Rule 2. Stop smiling so much, you goofs.

Does this look like the face of a victim? Of a follower?

Girls always tell me I need to smile more. Well, if girls think I am so ugly with my Mr. Frowny Face, why are they always talking to me and grabbing my arms and telling me how great my back feels when they hug me?

I smile when I'm around my goddaughters and my dog. Otherwise, I don't see any need to smile like some goof.

Rule 3. Show respect. Do not tolerate disrespect.

He is the nicest guy ever. Just don't piss him off. – Friend of Danger & Play

Civilization is a remarkable creation and we should respect it. Treat others with decency. Treat every person you meet with respect.

However, some people will mistake your respect for weakness. It is important to let people know that your kindness is not weakness.

If someone disrespects you (especially in that modern, passive-aggressive way), call them out on it. Ask them what their problem is. Tell them if they have a problem with you, then they need to be a man and explain what exactly their problem is so that you can be a man and work it out with them.

You can call people out respectfully. For example:

Bro, I'm not sure what you're getting at here. Maybe if you spell out your position then we'll find out that we have more in common than you think. But I need to know what you really mean before we can figure these things out. So... what exactly did you mean by that comment?

Give everyone a fair chance to prove that they are decent. If they are disrespectful, then there should be a problem.

Treat people with respect and do not tolerate disrespect and you'll be amazed how you develop social dominance. People will learn that you're the man to see when they want to confide in someone and that they should stay out of your way when they are being shady.

Passive-aggressive people will no longer be around you because they know that you'll call them out. Passive-aggressives hate being called out. Shine your light on the cockroaches and rats so that they will scurry far away from you.

Rule 4. Be nice.

All you have to do is follow three simple rules. One, never underestimate your opponent. Expect the unexpected. Two, take it outside. Never start anything inside the bar unless it's absolutely necessary. And three, be nice.

Some of you might wonder what being polite have to do with being dominant. That is because dominance has been given a bad name by reality TV shows like *Jersey Shore.*

Running around like a drunk idiot does not establish dominance. Being a rude idiot shows you lack self-respect and class. When you get too close to men like me, this is likely to happen.

Think about Hollywood leading men that are actually worth emulating. All are well-mannered. Can you imagine James Bond or the Most Interesting Man in the World being rude to a waitress?

Idiots from *Jersey Shore* aren't dominant. They are slaves to their emotions.

Jackals who walk slowly through crosswalks to show how "thug" and "street" they are aren't dominant men. They're cowards who have to travel in wolf packs and who are terrified when you get them alone.

Being nice and having good manners shows that you have some self-restraint; in other words, that you have some control over yourself.

Rule 5. Get Big. Be dangerous and playful. Learn a martial art.

Size is status. We are great apes. Never forget that.

Become a vanilla gorilla. People will move out of your way. People will be polite to you. People will assume you're a man of violence and treat you accordingly.

When you have size and strength and also know how to box or use Brazilian Jiu Jitsu, then you really are a force of nature.

Some of the toughest men I know are also very friendly and somewhat playful, even. They have no insecurity or fear because they know that when things pop off, they are prepared.

When you're a gorilla yet also polite and respectful, you'll be shocked at how quickly people warm to you. You are like the pit bull at the dog park that everyone is apprehensive of; when you're a little playful, people love you twice as much as they would otherwise.

Rule 6. Move with a purpose.

People tell me that I walk fast. I don't walk fast. I just don't walk aimlessly.

Do not shuffle your feet like some aimless sloth. If you have somewhere to be, then get there.

If you don't have anywhere to be, then lounge.

Rule 7. Lounge.

Don't stand when you can sit. Don't sit when you can lie down. Don't lie down when you can sleep.

When you're not moving with a purpose, lounge. Spread out like a lion in the savannah. Rest. Let your body heal. Being an alpha male is hard work.

Rule 8. Wear skull rings.

Skull rings are not merely corny PUA accessories. They are legal brass knuckles. If you know you're going into a shady area, "suit up."

Rule 9. Give your balls room to breathe.

In the jungle, space is status. If you occupy more space, you have more status. One easy way to remember to occupy more space is to ask if your balls are being crushed. That means your legs are too close together and that you aren't occupying enough space.

Rule 10. Check your testosterone levels.

Every study on evolutionary psychology has correlated testosterone levels with dominance. Every single study. It's not even debatable that testosterone is the dominance hormone.

A Tale of Two Men

Dave was an all-star football player in high school and voted best-dressed student. He was part of the cool crowd.

That's because, more than anything, Dave wanted to be cool. His self-image rested entirely on what others thought of him.

He followed all of the latest fashion trends and always had a hefty car payment, because he couldn't let anyone see him step outside of a Hyundai.

Dave spent hours at the night club meeting girls. Dave lost a weekend day or two of his life on hangovers and drug comedowns.

Dave worked for others, as he had no focus or purpose. His motivation was external. What do others think of me?

Dave never sat down in a room alone, away from all distractions, and asked what it meant to be a man.

He said he'd start his own business or make money online, but a man only has so many hours in the day.

He needed others to provide leadership for him and to feed his ego, which was always starving for approval. He won many awards for high performance. Yet he never felt satisfied or content. He never lived in the moment.

He met girls and actually had pretty good game. But because he lacked a sense of self, his women cheated on him.

Dave had a mid-life crisis and contemplated suicide.

Diligent Dan was a nobody. In some ways, he was the lowest of the losers.

Diligent Dan didn't start off with much. He had average genetics and wasn't voted most likely to succeed in high school.

He was the invisible man.

He followed the rules, went to college, and actually found a job after graduation.

Years later, he had trouble sleeping. Something inside him made him restless at night.

One day Dan was working his 9 to 5 when he spilled Starbucks coffee on his khakis. He jumped up instinctually when he caught a glimpse of his reflection on his monitor's screen.

"Is this all there is?" he wondered. He felt pent-up rage escaping from his pores.

The other cube rats looked at Dan with blank eyes. He felt like screaming, "Can't you see that we're all just human cattle?!"

His co-workers went back to work, their fingers moving up and down the keyboards like chickens pecking kernels of corn out of turds on the farmhouse floor.

Dan had been a brainwashed consumer and couldn't afford to quit his job, but he knew it was time to make a change.

Dan didn't know where to start, but he knew he had to make a move.

His daily routine changed. He would surf the web on the clock and type in "men's self-improvement."

He read success stories and his anger focused into something productive. Intensity. "What another man has done, I can do, too."

Dan embraced the suck.

He learned how to endure pain. He questioned his life purpose. Because his whole view of the world was proven to be a lie, he was overcome with anxiety and felt a pit in his stomach.

But he drove on.

Dan developed a dominant mindset.

He viewed his mind as a high performance sports car that would tolerate only the cleanest fuel. He turned off the television and meditated.

Dan learned what it meant to be treated with respect, as people understood that they would only enjoy Dan's company if they rose to his standards.

When people—even family and close friends—said negative things, he would get up, turn his back, and leave the room.

Dan no longer had the time to deal with whiners and complainers. He would help those who asked and lived by a new motto: "I don't have time for the slow or the weak."

Dan read that a man must have a strong body and a strong mind. He hit the weight room.

He didn't follow a specific program at first. He just went into the gym consistently and hit it hard.

Slowly, Dan's body transformed. His shirts fit a little bit tighter around his arms and shoulders and his pants were looser at the waist.

He had to buy new clothes after ripping his jeans out, as he couldn't find pants with a small waist and large quads.

He understood that his physical transformation was a metaphor for his entire life.

Dan was now a misfit of sorts, because he had overcome society's definition of manhood.

He felt pride in being a man, as he was always working towards his vision. He knew where he wanted to be. All of his existential angst dissipated.

He slept like a rock at night. He was excited to wake up in the morning and knew he needed a full night's sleep.

His confidence grew each day.

Occasionally, Dan was mistaken for a celebrity. "I've seen you before," people would insist. Dan would shrug his shoulders.

Women were showing up. Dan viewed women as a fun accessory to life, but always kept them at arm's length.

When women would try controlling him, he would let them know that they were and always would be second to his life purpose.

This made women love Dan even more.

Like a good little boy with a college degree, Dan was a filthy, godless atheist.

He questioned whether this world contained more than he could consciously perceive. People became attracted to him, as if a magnetic field or beam of light left his body. He became a sun that lit a dark world.

There were too many "coincidences." Dan would "coincidentally" run into people at the perfect time. It was as if his thoughts manifested themselves into the real world.

Randomly, a higher class of men found Dan and Dan found them. He didn't understand what was going on.

Dan would have an idea in his head of how much money he wanted to earn, and like magic the money would roll in.

Five years after that breakdown in his office, Dan had more money, more friends, and more women than he had time for.

He answered to no one and finally understood what it meant to be a free man.

There's a fork in the road, a choice to take.

Which man will you be?

Health and Fitness

Testosterone Biofeedback Roundtable: The Mind-Body Connection

(Gorilla Shrewdness #1)

As most of you know, I apply the scientific method to my self-improvement, whether that is in the gym, in relationships, or building this website. I formulate a hypothesis. I collect raw data. Whether it's blood work measuring my testosterone level or a DEXA scan, I share this data with you to see whether my results can work for you.

But I don't really go digging through the research to validate what I do. By my own admission, my experiments could be attacked on grounds that "anecdotal evidence is anecdotal." My approach serves my purpose to get you guys actionable information that I have used myself and I believe can work for you. However, I know some of you also like more scientific theory and research support as well.

That is why I was pleased to meet Dr. Jeremy Nicholson. Some of you may have already seen his article here on D&P about the science behind posture and mindset increasing testosterone, or have been to his *Attraction Doctor* blog on *Psychology Today.*

For those who don't know, Dr. Jeremy is a social/personality psychologist who focuses on dating and relationships, as well as social influence. He is also interested in all kinds of self-improvement for men (that's how we connected). Dr. Jeremy takes the complementary approach to what I do in his advice, though; he starts with scientific theory and research. He looks at principles, concepts, and experimental results. He uses that as a foundation to provide solutions to people for dating and relationships, self-improvement, and business, too.

Despite our different approaches, we met in the middle over common goals and interests. So, I invited him to what may be the first of many roundtable discussions. A discussion between professional, masculine men. A meeting of fellow "Gorillas"... Gorilla Shrewdness.

Our first roundtable discussion will cover the biofeedback that occurs between your HTPA and the rest of your body.

A reader asks:
"I'm curious though: why do these exercises boost your testosterone more than just a normal kind of workout? Like squats or normal dead lifts or whatever? Is it mainly because of the posture?"

<u>Mike Says:</u>

Here are my thoughts, Dr. Jeremy. Tell me what you think. In evolution, "space is status." There is a lot of research showing that a decline of status is associated with depression and other negative life outcomes. As animals, we are horrified of losing space.

Loss aversion is explained by the first principle that "space is status." (Loss aversion is a principle from behavioral economics. Experiments have shown that people fear losses far more than they value gains. As the saying goes, "Losing feels worse than winning feels good.")

As animals, the amount of space we occupy determines whether we live or die. A lion who loses space is going to be kicked out of the pride or killed by new challengers.

The end of an alpha leaves a bloody mess: https://www.youtube.com/watch?v=n7Sq-SJmd5Y

My theory is that our body is hardwired to release hormones relative to our status.

Indeed, as this excellent TED talk by Amy Cuddy on body language shows, my theory is becoming accepted by visionary thinkers:

If we are low status, then our body will not want to release testosterone, because it may cause us to engage in acts that challenge the alpha male: acts that could get us killed.

Our hypothalamic–pituitary–gonadal axis (HTPA) can sense when we are high status or low status based on our body posture. When we are taking up more space, our body releases testosterone. When we take up less space, our bodies release more cortisol.

Dr. Jeremy Says:
Mike… you bring up a number of good points.

Much of what you suggest has been supported for 30 years or more by research on primates (including us humans).

For example, in 1985, Mazer published an article discussing how biology, behavior, and social status interact in primate groups. The summary of that paper says:

"This paper describes a biosocial model of status in face-to-face groups. It argues that status ranks are allocated among members of a group through face-to-face interaction and that the allocation process is similar across each primate species, including humans. Every member of a group signifies its rank through physical or vocal demeanor. For

*example, behavioral signs of dominant status include erect posture,
glares, eye contact, strutting, and (in humans) assertive speech.
Individuals whose behaviors exhibit dominance show high or rising
levels of testosterone compared to those who exhibit deference.
Testosterone and dominance are reciprocally related. The model relies
more on research on males than on females. It is proposed as a theory
about both sexes, but with a caution that little is known about sex
differences in the relation of hormones to dominance behavior."*

Essentially then, dominant behaviors, status/power in a social
group, and testosterone levels all reciprocally influence one
another.

To get back to the reader's question more directly though,
there is certainly a benefit of any type of anabolic exercise on
endocrine function. I believe that the postural exercises that Mike
suggests may have added benefit in two ways:

1. Good posture itself may have an effect. Having an open,
upright, and relaxed posture may simply help the body function
overall. At the least, such postures can promote relaxation, which
decreases stress/cortisol and can therefore increase testosterone. A
study by Carney, Cuddy, and Yap (2010), which I mentioned in
the article about the science of posture and testosterone, did find a
reduction in cortisol for participants who posed in powerful
postures. Therefore, the effect Mike is getting with these exercises
may be some kind of structural alignment or even relaxation
response type of phenomenon.

2) Dominant body language also has a reciprocal relationship
with emotions. For example, when we are happy, we smile. BUT,
if we force ourselves to hold a smile, we will also become happier
(Zajonc, Murphy, & Inglehart, 1989). In much the same way as a
smile affects mood, powerful body language may also be helping
to create positive emotions and an assertive mindset. In support of
that idea, the study I cited above by Carney, Cuddy, and Yap

(2010) also found that participants striking high-power postures felt significantly more powerful and in charge, compared to low-power posturing peers, and were also more focused on rewards.

Such psychological states, in turn, may relate to other neuroendocrine changes. Thus, we may also be seeing a "fake it until you make it" type effect on mindset and emotion, leading to greater testosterone production as well.

In either case, the main benefit of such postures is that they can be done routinely/constantly. Practicing such body language and mindset can result in them being chronically activated. Therefore, rather than getting a temporary increase from a workout or a victory, such exercises may allow for regulation of testosterone over a longer time frame. After all, the research I discussed in the science of posture and testosterone article—about changes in testosterone levels in men during marriage and divorce—seems to indicate longer-term effects on testosterone due to psychological and social changes (Mazur & Booth, 1998).

In short then, the added benefit of these exercises may come from the fact that they help to relax the body, promote good behavioral habits, and/or improve mindset and emotions, in order to better regulate testosterone levels over the long term. In other words, this is not simply "performing an exercise," but rather developing the habit of functioning in a physiologically and psychologically powerful, masculine way.

Of course, all of this is an educated hypothesis, based on the results of other studies. Additional testing would be necessary to tease apart a more specific "why" among all of these reciprocal relationships. Mike's personal results, however, certainly serve as a good case study to support that these longer-term effects are taking place by at least one of these paths... if not more.

References:

• Carney, D.R., Cuddy, A.J.C., Yap, A.J. (2010). Power posing: Brief nonverbal displays affect neuroendocrine levels and risk tolerance. Psychological Science, 21, 1363-1368.

• Mazer, A. (1985). A biosocial model of status in face-to-face primate groups. Social Forces, 64, 377-402.

• Mazur, A., & Booth, A. (1998). Testosterone and dominance in men. Behavioral and Brain Sciences, 21, 353-397.

• Zajonc, R. B., Murphy, S. T. & Inglehart, M. (1989). Feeling and facial efference: Implications for the vascular theory of emotion. Psychological Review, 96, 395-416.

Going from Fit to Big

My body has undergone some interesting changes over the past few years. I've gone from fat to fit and then from fit to big(ish). I'm currently on track to get an elite physique, which will take me another 2-3 years or so. While going from fit to big, I've noticed quite a few interesting things.

What do I mean by "fit" v. "big?" When you're fit, you get these awesome gym pumps and look amazing... for about 60 minutes. Then your muscles sort of deflate. Your look also fluctuates greatly depending upon whether you've had enough carbs, whether you are hydrated, etc.

Once you pass a certain threshold, you always look like you have size. You can tell that I train even when fully clothed, where as a fit person needs to take some clothes off before people can tell you spend a lot of time in the gym.

(The difference between being fit and being big is that you don't need to take your clothes off or wear tank tops for people to know you train.)

Now although I'm big(ish), my body isn't where it needs to be. I need to put on another 10-20 pounds of muscle before I'll be happy with it.

Yes, women find you more attractive. Let's just get this out of the way. I don't care about that "scientific study" that allegedly shows that the ideal physique that women more desire is Brad Pitt's from *Fight Club.* In the real world, I go by what women do and not how they answer survey questions.

I've been fit and big. I know what women find attractive. I know how to read what the nerds call indicators of interest.

You simply get more IOIs from women. That's just the way it is. If you disagree with me and have never been on both sides of the fence, then you don't have the right to an opinion. In short, I don't want to hear any garbage from Internet nerds about what women want.

No, it's not about confidence. Some will say, "It's not that you're bigger that draws more attention. It's that being big makes you more confident, and this in turn translates to more attraction from women."

No. I am a confident mofo and have always been confident. When you have the experience I have with women along with the ability to know you can beat up most guys, you have a certain swag.

I don't really understand a lot of you guys. You read all of these books on evolutionary psychology like *Sperm Wars* and quote them like gospel. Well, what is so hard to understand about this?

We are apes. In the jungle, size is king. Women like big men. That's just evolution.

In the wild, everyone wants to be around the biggest ape and the biggest lion. In the human world, women want to be around the biggest men. It's primal, it's hard-wired, and it's reality.

Women will outright grab you. At my birthday party, a girl came up from behind, grabbed me and said, "I know you! We met earlier today!" McQueen was there and witnessed it, so this is not Internet B.S. I had to shake her off as she wouldn't let go.

There is no doubt that I could have taken her to my car within five minutes of meeting her. It wasn't because of my "game." It was raw animal sexuality.

And it's not like that was the first time a girl has sexually assaulted me. Girls regularly grab my bicep and often they push their boobs up against my back even when there is ample room to pass by without touching me.

Men want to talk to you more. If I'm just sitting around minding my own business, a guy will come up and make conversation with me. They don't even always bring up training.

They just want to be around bigger guys. I don't know why. It's just something primal in us.

Men also assume that if you're big, it's because you have your act together. I just met a VP from a big bank the other day. He just came to shoot the shit. He was a really cool guy and we might end up partying together in Cabo this spring.

If I had been a skinny guy, he never would have noticed me.

You get more attention from the Bad Ass Bitches. What is the difference between hot and Bad Ass Bitch? I can't say, but we all know them when we see them. There is a certain look to them that differs from girls who are merely hot or highly attractive.

People touch you more. Now, I've been around long enough to know when a girl is grabbing me in a sexual way and when she's just curious. I also lived in San Francisco's SOMA district (second gayest neighborhood other than Castro) and know when a gay man is making the moves on me.

My dermatologist is a 75-year old man without a gay bone in his body. When I was standing up at the counter to pay, he walked by me and sort of "jocked" me in a non-gay way. When girls you know hug you, they will physically squeeze you. Again, this is non-sexual.

You get better customer service. "The squeaky wheel gets the grease," and by virtue of being big, people think you are angry and mean. I just got a free cup of hand-crafted coffee for, in the words of the hipster barista, "waiting in line quietly and patiently."

I could talk about stereotyping and note that I am cultured, have travelled all over the world, and am widely read. But if people want to give me free stuff because they expect me to smash things, who cares?

You look more regal. If you were putting up some statues in your front office, you wouldn't put gazelles or giraffes up there. You'd put something big and badass; lions, apes, wolves, etc.

As human beings, we're attracted to large physical bodies. **Being bigger is better in every conceivable way**. There is likely a point where you're "too big." I am bigger than 90% of men and yet I am not even close to being "too big."

I have several friends who are bigger than I am and they haven't reached that point. Keep striving to get bigger and you will be handsomely rewarded with more attention from women, better customer service, more money, and more friends.

Increasing Muscular Density and Muscle Tone

For years I had a nice body… when at the gym. After loading my body up with NO boosters, creatine, and beta alanine, I was a beast.

Outside of the gym, once the pump went away, my body really wasn't where it needed to be. (That changed once I went from fit to big.)

I lacked muscular density.

Muscular density refers to the hardness your muscles have when at rest. Muscular density is also referred to as *muscle tone:*

"In physiology, medicine, and anatomy, muscle tone (residual muscle tension or tonus) is the continuous and passive partial contraction of the muscles, or the muscle's resistance to passive stretch during resting state."

Everyone can have big muscles when the blood is pumped up with blood, nitric oxide, BCAAs, and creatine.

But unless you're doing push-ups at the club, a body lacking muscular density isn't going to do you much good. I needed to find a way to always look big and to have a body that women want.

There are two great ways to increase your muscular density.

You need to start doing static holds and 1-and-1/3 reps so that you can get a thick, dense look.

Static holds. When I first started training static holds, I changed my body over the summer. Although I didn't gain any weight, I looked bigger. I immediately had my friend start doing static holds. His body changed in a couple of my months and he looked bigger at 168 pounds than most guys look at 200. (Most people assume I weigh 20 pounds more than I actually do.)

Here's how to do static holds: during your last work set of a major muscle group (chins, bench, dips, etc.), hold the weight at the top of the movement. Fight the movement for 30-60 seconds. When training friends I actually countdown aloud: 30, 29, 28…

Imagine you are doing a pull-up. At the top of the movement, hold it. Gravity is going to keep pulling on your body. Fight gravity for as long as possible.

Your muscles will continue contracting while you are holding yourself on the chin-up bar.

At the top of the squat or deadlift, don't just rack the bar when your set is complete. Slightly bend the knees and support the weight.

The takeaway is to get your muscle fibers contracting while *sustaining* a load, not just when moving a load through a range of motion. Today I did a hellacious static hold/ab workout.

Raise yourself to the top position of a chin-up. Do leg lifts while holding your chin over the bar. Brutal.

"Unconscious nerve impulses maintain the muscles in a partially contracted state. If a sudden pull or stretch occurs, the body responds by automatically increasing the muscle's tension, a reflex which helps guard against danger as well as helping to maintain balance. Such near-continuous innervation can be thought of as a 'default' or 'steady state' condition for muscles. There is, for the most part, no actual 'rest state' insofar as activation is concerned."

1-and-1/3 reps.

Most reps are "down-up." You lower the weight in the bench press. You press the weight. One rep. Down-up.

- **Bench press/pushing movements**: To do a 1-and-1/3 rep, you lower the weight in the bench press all the way to your chest. You press the barbell 1/3 of the way up. Then you lower it again. Then you do one full range of motion repetition.

Each rep is thus more than one rep. It's one-and-one-third of a rep. Do 5-7 of these reps.

- **Rows/pulling movements**: The 1-and-1/3 rep works best for back. Do a cable row. At the top of the movement (you have the weight pulled back at your body), let the weight go 1/3 of the way back. Pull the weight back towards. Then let the weight go all the way down. Then pull the bar back towards your body.

Doing 1-and-1-1/3 reps will ensure that your back remains contracted throughout the entire movement.

I know guys who never got a pump in their rear lats whose back growth exploded after adding 1-and-1/3 reps.

Although this method works best for the back, you can do 1-and-1/3 reps for other exercises.

You can also vary where you add the 1/3 rep. Maybe you are stronger at the bottom of the bench press and weaker at the top of the movement. In that case, do not lower the weight all the way to your chest.

Instead you should lower the weight 1/3 of the way towards your chest. Then press the weight up. Then do your full repetition.

How to add static holds and 1-and-1/3 reps into your training.

Static holds can be hell on your joints, so use them with caution. Start off with 10-second holds and work your way up.

You don't need to do static holds for every movement. Just pick one major movement for your large body parts. I do static holds for T-bar rows, pull-ups, and the hammer strength chest machine.

I don't advise using static holds for free weight movements like the bench press or shoulder press. Your neural system may give out, causing you to dump the weight. Ask yourself, "If I dumped the weight, would it fall on my head?" If so, don't do a static hold.

Avoid using static holds for smaller muscle groups, as they will wreck your biceps tendon.

1-and-1/3 reps are much easier on your joints. I even use a form of 1-and-1/3 reps for my biceps.

21s (biceps curls)

Start at the top of the movement and lower the bar one-third of the way. Do seven reps.
Start at the bottom of the movement and raise the bar one-third of the way. Do seven reps.
Do seven full reps.

Start incorporating static holds and 1-and-1/3 reps and within eight weeks you will notice a major improvement in how your body looks while at rest.

How I Train

A lot of guys ask how I train and ask for my "program."

I have some news that will make Internet nerds throughout the world blow a gasket.

I don't follow a workout program at all.

But doesn't that violate the principle of progressive overload!? How will you ever make specific adaptations to imposed demands if you just… go out and… do whatever?!
(Beats me.)

I have fun and love being in the gym. I'm a straight up gym rat.

If my body could handle it, I would be in the gym for three hours a day, seven days a week.

I love everything about being at the gym. No, not like: *love*.

I love when the sun is out and they open up the garage doors at Gold's in Venice. I love seeing the huge bodybuilders train. (Rich Piana trains at Gold's.)

I love seeing men 20 years older than I am who look jacked as hell and put me to shame. It reminds me that age is just a number and to step up my game for the next few *decades* to come.

I love seeing women in yoga pants and sports bras doing stiff-legged dead lifts.

I love how women unconsciously lick their lips when I walk by. They objectify me and treat me like a piece of meat.

I don't need to be motivated or inspired to go to the gym. I need to be motivated to leave the gym and actually get some income-producing work done.

Carrying around a log book and agonizing over every detail would take the fun away.

(For men like Big George, analyzing the data is part of the fun, and that's totally cool.)

I'm not going to ever be on a stage and don't care to be. I don't train like a bodybuilder.

My way wouldn't work for a competitive bodybuilder. I have no desire to ever compete.

I have no desire to be cracked out on stimulants because I'm not eating and then be moody and lose my mind.

Or to weigh food.

I don't like the limelight.

I don't even like posting my pictures online.

I have to because of all the frauds out there.

You need to know you can trust me.

I'm on Instagram now. It'll be a sort of exercise library and recipe book with a dose of swag.

My training is half-bodybuilder, half athletic.

Let's take a leg day:

- Foam roll/trigger point therapy.
- I'll do some box jumps.
- Then I'll do a slow, grinding, 20-rep squat (using a machine!), HIT style.
- Then some Romanian deadlifts with kettle bells. Kettle bells have fat handles, so I'm training my grip with "fat bar" type training and working my posterior chain. Multiple sets of 15-20.
- Then some leg curls on a machine, HIT style.

45

- Finish with some Farmer's Walks.
- Then push the Prowler.

Some days I just do whatever.

Today, it was sunny at Gold's in Venice. I wanted to train in the outdoor area. I went out there, looked around to see what equipment was available, and made up a workout.

- Pushed the prowler on the high bars and low bars.
- Did farmer's walks with a trap-bar.
- Hula hoops. (Yes, I'm serious.)
- Dead lifts with a trap bar.
- Jumped rope with my new jump rope.

I didn't weigh the trap bar to see how many pounds I was lifting. I didn't time my sets. I didn't count my steps.
Then I went inside:

- Reverse hypers.
- Sitting leg curls.
- Leg extensions.

I didn't watch the clock to see if my cortisol levels were going to spike because I had been lifting for over an hour.
I just did.
I broke a sweat, got some Vitamin D, and enjoyed the hell out of my afternoon.

My nutrition is a mess, too.

I went to my alpha kitchen, made a bowl of alpha chili, found some tortilla chips, and then ate a few spoons full of ice cream.

I didn't have a panic attack about the "anabolic, post-workout window" that requires me to take 100 mg of maltodextrin along with "fast absorbing whey protein."

Right now I'm at the Coffee Bean & Tea Leaf drinking a no-sugar-added chai latte with almond-coconut milk while writing this post.

Whatever.

Later on, I'll eat some more chili and some Quest protein bars, coming in at the day at around 3,000 kcals, plus or minus 500.

I enjoy the heck out of life. I don't agonize over log books or count calories.

Here's a magic diet for you to follow.

When I'm a little too soft, I make sure I'm hungry throughout the day. If I'm hungry, then I'm losing fat. No, I don't count calories.

If I'm too weak to train, then my cals are too low, so I'll have a beet juice with BCAAs before and during my training session.

There you have it.

Seems to be working. Girls like me.

I don't have to tell people I "work out" all of the time or carry around a gallon jug of water to prove that I really do go to the gym!

How can you get super jacked and ripped?

I'd follow the exact same "program" I currently follow.

Except I would add to my current TRT dose of 150-200 mgs of test:

- 300 mg testosterone/week

- 300 mg trenbolone/week
- 300 mg masteron/week
- T3/T4
- (ECA stack or Clen)

Same program, same design, same principles + more gear = 20 pounds of lean body mass.

I'd play with carb depletion, mess with sodium, get some pictures taken, and pretend that's how I look year round.

Even though I don't have a program, I do have principles.

Those will be discussed on a later day. Yes, there is a right way and wrong way to structure your workout.

That's how I train and eat.

It's not for everybody.

Many people like structure.

You will never get super-shredded doing it, since your body starts going insane as you approach (and hold) 10% body fat.

But it works for me.

What Kind of Body Do Women Want?

A topic of tiresome and endless debate exists over a simple question: what kind of body do women want a man to have?

It's a silly debate because there is no right answer. There are six right answers.

Which is the holy grail of bodies? Unless you have a good body and are looking to take it to the next level, arguing over this stuff just makes you a keyboard warrior.

Lift some weights, don't be so fat that you float in a swimming pool, don't be so skinny the wind will blow you over, and women will be OK with your body.

Once you have a body that women are starting to find themselves attracted to, then you've earned the right to argue about what is the best body for attracting women. Until then, hit the gym hard. Once you get a decent body, you'll learn from first-hand experience what body women find the sexiest.

Juicing Basics, Juicing Recipes and ANDI Juices

It's hard to know what to begin juicing (assuming you have a juicer). The best way to begin is with what I call the "working man's juice."

In the South, an RC Cola and a Moon Pie were known as the working man's lunch. Working people wanted something that would provide quick energy while tasting good. The "working man's lunch" appealed to everyone.

The hardest thing about getting people to drink juice is getting them to drink juice. Everyone expects a juice to be nasty. You see a lot of pursed lips, scrunched noses, and squinting eyes.

"What's in this, man?"

This juice will appeal to everyone, and is basically the entry point into juice:

- 4 carrots
- 1 apple
- 1 small piece (size of your pinky finger tip) ginger

Everyone likes that juice. Whenever a person has the above juice, he or she says, "Oh, that's not bad."

It's actually really good, but expectations influence taste perception. People expect the juice to taste like grass clippings. The carrot-apple-ginger juice is so good that it overcomes the anti-juice bias.

From there you should start reducing the sweet content and start increasing the vegetable content. For example:

- 3 carrots

- ½ apple
- 3 large leaves of kale, romaine, or some other green
- ginger

Eventually, you'll want to increase the greens to as much as you can tolerate and decrease the sweet fruits and vegetables.

After you've had some beginner's juices, you can start making your own. To make your own juices, think of combining three bases: green water, vegetables, greens, and fruits.

A green water is a vegetable that gives off a lot of water. Celery, zucchini, broccoli, cucumber, bok choy, and cabbage all provide a lot of green water per pound of produce. (That is, they have a high yield.) They are also low in sugar.

Leafy greens are kale, Swiss chard, collard greens, spinach, red lettuce, and other nutrient rich, dense, greens. Greens do have what's called a high yield; that is, it doesn't give much juice per pound of produce. So you don't want to make greens your base.

The sweet base is fruits and sweet vegetables like carrots and beets. Carrots and beets have a really high yield.

Giving recipes is hard because as you juice, your tastes will change. You'll want more carrots or apples in your juice today than you'll want a year from now. My juices might be too green for you.

But.

There's no wrong way to juice. Keep adding stuff, tasting it along the way, and you'll find out the right ratios.

Now you just get all mad scientist in the kitchen.

Here's what I juiced this week:

Beet, kale, ginger juice
- 1 medium beet (beets will turn your urine and stools red; no cause for alarm)
- 6 whole kale leaves + stems

- 1" ginger

Bok Choy Ginger Lemonade
- 6 bok choy leaves + stems
- 3 small lemons (I always remove the skin; others leave it on for zest)
- 1" ginger

Beet, carrot, kale, ginger juice
- 1 medium sized beet
- 3 carrots
- 5 whole kale leaves + stems
- 1" ginger

Cabbage carrot juice
- 1 whole cabbage
- 6 carrots
- 1" ginger

Swiss chard lemonade
- 1 bunch Swiss chard
- 4 small lemons
- add sparkling water

Cabbage grapefruit juice
- 1 whole cabbage
- 2 grapefruits
- 1 apple

Celery refresher
- 6 stalks celery
- 3 lemons
- 1 bunch parsley

Pineapple kale juice
- 2 cups pineapple (remove rind)
- 6 large kale leaves and stems

Kale lemonade
- 6 large kale leaves and stems
- 4 lemons
- 1 apple
- Sparkling water

As you can see, I especially enjoy citrus fruits. Just start from the premise that you want more greens and less fruit and you'll end up in the right place.

Also, try juicing as many ANDI score foods as you can.

ANDI is short for **Aggregate Nutrient Density Index**. The ANDI score is based on a food's content of calcium, beta carotene, alpha carotene, lutein & zeaxanthin, lycopene, fiber, folate, glucosinolates, iron, magnesium, niacin, selenium, vitamin B1 (thiamin), vitamin B2 (riboflavin), vitamin B6, vitamin B12, vitamin C, vitamin E, zinc, and the food's ORAC. (Oxygen Radical Absorbance Capacity measures how many free radicals a food will "destroy.")

"1000" is a perfect score, and any score over 100 is very good for you.

Top ANDI Foods to Juice

1. Collard, mustard, & turnip greens 1000
2. Kale 1000
3. Watercress 1000
4. Bok choy 824

5. Spinach 739
6. Brussels sprouts 672
7. Swiss chard 670
8. Arugula 559
9. Radish 554
10. Cabbage 481
11. Red peppers 420
12. Romaine lettuce 389
13. Broccoli 376
14. Carrot 344
15. Tomatoes & tomato products 190-300
16. Cauliflower 295
17. Strawberries 212
18. Pomegranate 193
19. Blackberries 178
20. Raspberries 145
21. Blueberries 130
22. Papaya 118
23. Oranges 109

Relationships and Dating

4 Ways to Make People Like You

Let's be real. "Be true to yourself" is a nice slogan, but in the real world, there comes a time when we need people to like us. It's only human nature to want people to like you. The problem is that no one actually taught you how to make people like you.

I will show you how to make people like you.

But remember the first line? We are being real.

This is going to require an immense amount of work by you.

If you're not willing to put the work in, close the browser and stop reading.

This isn't stuff I made up. These are principles I've applied in the real world and that are backed by science. Part 1 contains the science behind the recommendations. Part 2 is the nuts and bolts application of the scientific principles.

Don't just read this post. Bookmark it.
Read it and study it and apply and practice everything I'm about to show you.

If you don't like social science or technical jargon, scroll down out the second half of the article to the section titled **The 4 Specific Ways to Make People Like You**. Otherwise, read on.

The most concise research paper I've been able to find provides a simple—well, four simple—ways to become more likable. See *Why Are Narcissists so Charming at First Sight? Decoding the Narcissism–Popularity Link at Zero Acquaintance*. (You can read the full paper here.)

"Zero acquaintance" means that researchers showed a picture to some people and then asked those people to make guesses about personality. The test subjects didn't get to meet the person in the photograph.

It shows what we've already known about women (and people in general), but it actually contains actionable advice once you decode it.

Acting like a narcissist will make people like you.

Wait a second! Narcissists are evil, aren't they!?

Maybe so, if you haven't gone beyond good and evil.

Yet everyone seems to like narcissists. Watch *Mad Men*. Women love Don Draper, who uses rough sex techniques that feminists decry but women love.

You can be a McDork who seethes with envy because you *can't believe she is with that guy*. Or you can make people like you. The choice, as always, is yours.

People are drawn to narcissists like bears to honey.

Is the sweetness worth the sting? Yes, it is. The findings are clear on two points.

1. People can identify narcissists.
2. People are still drawn to narcissists.

1. People are darned good at spotting narcissists.

Yes, stereotypes are true. Trust your gut. If someone looks like a narcissist to you, he probably is. "Recent findings also show that narcissism is detectable at zero acquaintance. Observers thus seem to like narcissists at first sight, although they accurately perceive their narcissism."

Look at a picture of Jordan Belfort. You've never met him (i.e., you're at "zero acquaintance").

Yet you can tell he's a narcissist even if you hadn't seen *The Wolf of Wall Street.*

All you need to do is look at a picture. "Specifically for narcissism, researchers have shown that observers are able to judge targets' narcissism on the basis of full-body photographs."

In fact, more information does not usually prove your guts wrong. "These findings parallel research on the accuracy of personality judgments based on thin slices of the targets' behaviors and physical appearances. In many cases, <u>the accuracy of snap judgments only increases slightly when based on more information</u>."

2. People love narcissists.

Since you can look at a picture and tell if someone is a narcissist, then you're going to hate the person. Right? Nope. That's exactly wrong. In fact, "Narcissists indeed make a positive impression on strangers."

It gets more interesting, as researchers found that, "the aspects of narcissism that are most maladaptive in the long run (exploitativeness/entitlement) proved to be most attractive at zero acquaintance." Read that again.

And again.

And again.

Until you finally get it.

"The aspects of narcissism that are most maladaptive in the long run proved to be most attractive."

Now let's get to the good stuff. How can <u>YOU</u> become more liked?

The researchers found that, "an examination of observable verbal and nonverbal behaviors as well as aspects of physical appearance provided an explanation for why narcissists are more popular at first sight."

The 4 Specific Ways to Make People Like You

The study showed that, "Narcissism was related to <u>fancier clothing</u>, a <u>more charming facial expression</u>, more <u>self-assured body movements</u>, and more <u>verbal humor</u>, all of which led to popularity."

Yes, this is going to take some work on your appearance. You are worth it!

1. Wear fancier clothing.

Yes, fashion matters. You can't wear baggy jeans—called *dad jeans* for a reason—and expect women or other men to like and respect you.

Become the man to see. Check out my 5 Fashion Rules for Men. Learn how to look nice while on a budget. Listen to my introverts and game podcast for some more fashion tips.

2. Use more charming facial expressions.

Learn how to furrow your eyebrows. Make goofy faces to crack little kids up. It's the best practice you'll ever get, because children are honest. If they don't laugh, you're not funny. "Wine and children speak the truth."

Eye contact is huge. Use your eyes when playing with your kids or nieces and nephews. Learn how to shut a little kid down with a look. (We all remember *that* look, right? Master it.)

Read this book on body language to understand how to read and make your own facial cues. The Body Language book is great to keep on your coffee table or desk and skim.

When you're reading to go deep into the subject, check out *Emotions Revealed: Recognizing Faces and Feelings to Improve Communication and Emotional Life.*

Watching *Mad Men* is a rare time when television isn't for losers. Look at Don Draper's facial expressions and his deadpan humor. Study him like a cultural anthropologist would study a tribal leader.

3. Use alpha body language and make self-assured body movements.

How can you develop self-assured body movement? I cover that in "Move and Live With Purpose."

Check out my "How to Become a More Dominant Man" series in the Masculinity chapter if you haven't already.

Watch this TED talk on how to use alpha body language. (Bonus: using alpha male body language can naturally raise your testosterone level.)

Get big. When you're big, you don't need to play around with silly alpha male poses. You naturally take up space simply by existing.

Space is status.

If you're a big man with dense muscles, your body language will naturally be more alpha. Don't skip back day, as getting a big back is the single best way to have natural alpha male body language.

4. Use verbal humor.

Watch these three videos of Arnold on the *Tonight Show with Johnny Carson*. Notice how he uses humor to diffuse hostile situations. Study them.

There is no better source of how to use verbal humor as an alpha male than Arnold videos. There are dozens of them on YouTube. Watch them all.

Arnold Schwarzenegger: Women Can Weightlift to Get Fit, Part 1 of 3, Johnny Carson
https://www.youtube.com/watch?v=Y4OXujrjcRk

Arnold Schwarzenegger Make Exercise & Goal Setting Part of Life, Part 2 of 3, Johnny Carson
https://www.youtube.com/watch?v=5CUG06OOE0A

Arnold Schwarzenegger, Exercise 20 Minutes per Day, Part 3 of 3, Johnny Carson's Tonight Show
https://www.youtube.com/watch?v=A2AiLbpkngA

Apply Those 4 Principles and People Will Love You Even When They Know They Shouldn't

Yes, actually apply the principles. Read the sources I cited. Watch the videos.

Don't just nod your head in agreement and say, "Cool article, bro, I totally agree with everything you wrote."

Step 1. Bookmark this post. Refer to it often.

Step 2. Choose an area you are lacking in.

Step 3. Focus on that area.

Step 4. Get a mirror and practice making facial expressions in front of the mirror. Practice your body language poses in front of the mirror.

Step 5. Share your successes and struggles.

Become the Man to See

I had finished a long workweek when one of my girls called me, begging me to come out. "I'm tired," I told her, and had in any event just taken some sleeping pills.

"I'm going to bed."

"No, please come out."

"Why?"

"I want to be seen with you."

Women increase their status with other women by presenting a high-value man. She really wanted me to come out, because it would have impressed the girls she was with. It would have made her seem more valuable, because she was with me.

My life mindset is to be the man I want to be. My game mindset is to be the kind of man women want to be seen with.

When you leave the house, you should be asking yourself: *right now*, do I look like the kind of man an attractive woman would want to be seen with? If you look slovenly, with a bad haircut and Old Navy jeans, why would you expect a woman to be receptive to your approach?

Women talk non-stop about relationships, and every woman wants to be able to "brag on" her man. If you are the kind of man a woman wants to talk to her friends about, then you will have more women than you can handle.

Guys need to realize that women do not live in the same world as we do. As a man, I don't care if my friends or complete strangers on the street find my girls attractive. I care if my girl makes me hard, will fuck whenever I want, and will please me in the bedroom.

Although most guys are not as extreme as I am—that is, guys want "arm candy" to some extent—we are much less worried about what our friends think of the women we date. Think about it.

How many times have you railed a chick of low-quality, knowing your friends would ridicule you the next morning? Did thinking "my friends are going to mess with me" actually stop you from getting the bang? Of course not. You went for it anyway, and then took your lumps like a 'G.

Women have an entirely different mindset. To a woman, what her friends will think is more important than what she thinks. One might even say that women are incapable of thinking for themselves, but instead are part of a hive mind.

If you look like a slob with a bad haircut who is wearing Old Navy clothing, why would a woman want to be seen with you? If you are a do-nothing, boring guy with no life story, why would you be someone she'd want to talk about?

Far more important than new pick-up openers or routines is looking like a man women want to be seen with.

Gaining 10 pounds of muscle, losing fat, and finding your look will do far more to improve your game than the latest "social dynamics" DVD's.

If you want to meet women, first become a man worth meeting.

10 Ways to Not Get Laid

Find fault in every girl. The pretty blonde with a great smile and huge tits? Her feet are big. The brunette with a pedicure is probably a redneck. Spare yourself the possibility of being rejected by lying to yourself, "None of these girls are good enough. I'll just wait until someone who meets my standards walks in."

Stand in a corner of the bar. Women who see you will wonder, "Who is that sexy mystery man standing alone?" They won't think that a guy (or, even better, a group of guys) standing on the outside looking in is pathetic.

Wait for a girl to give you permission before approaching her. Agonize over whether she is twirling her hair because she is flirting with you or because its really getting in her eyes.

Overthink and analyze everything. Even though there are 52 Fridays in a year and you will probably be going out for 10 years, going out is a super-serious event. Meeting women deserves all of the seriousness of thought that investing in the stock market or buying your first home requires. Be sure to constantly furrow your brow as you analyze the night's data. Get really angry if something goes wrong.

Be fat. You always see "PUAs" wearing shiny shirts with the hottest women, right? Only losers who haven't read the latest PUA Action Alert go to the gym, eat clean foods, and juice.

Treat venue selection like a committee meeting. Argue with three other guys about venues. Drag this out as long as possible. "Let's have another beer while we decide." Throwing good money after bad has always been a viable business strategy and so it makes total sense to spend more time at a bar everyone agrees sucks.

Don't roll solo/always roll out in big groups. Only losers go out alone. A girl might ask you, "Where are your friends?" Having the ability to move to a new bar that better suits you is overrated. It makes far more sense to argue with 3 other guys over the next venue to hit up.

Don't make guy friends. Even though you are at the same bar with the same phone doing the same thing as thousands of other people, tell yourself that you are better than they are. They are losers. You are *too fucking cool*. That guy couldn't possibly be interesting, even though by being in the same place and same time as you, you are actually that guy.

Do not make eye contact. Only creeps look into another person's eyes.

Do not be the kind a man a woman would be proud to have her friends see her with. Having a nice haircut, wearing clean clothes, and looking fresh? That's for homos. You'll wear your polo shirt and cargo shorts. Like a boss.

Follow the above ten tips and I guarantee that you won't get laid.

How Do I Get Out of the Friend Zone?

How do I get out of the friend zone? I will tell you in less than five minutes how to get out of the friend zone, although you might not like my answer. You likely never had a strong male role model in your life who told you that men and women aren't designed to be friends.

1. You're not her friend.

You want to sleep with her. Be honest about your intentions. If she were fat and disgusting, you wouldn't be "friends" with her. Stop lying to yourself and stop lying to me. You're not her friend.

2. She's not your friend.

She is using you as a free psychotherapist. Friends help each other out. When has your "friend" helped you get laid, helped you moved, or put your own interests above her own?

3. Stop waiting around for table scraps like a vulture.

Other men are getting all up in that like she's Miss Teen Delaware and you're doing what… waiting for them to finish? Have some self-respect.

Being in the friend zone means you need a mindset adjustment.

Be a lion, not a vulture.

4. Go build a crew of legit men.

Men and women are not evolved to "hang out." Men are hunters and women are gatherers.

Men take action, women chew the fat.

Stop blabbing for hours about emotional crap with women.

Go find other hunters.

Charisma and Connection

Charisma can be learned.

How do you develop charisma? It helps to examine charismatic people like Bill Clinton, Arnold Schwarzenegger, and Tony Robbins. What do they do that you don't do? What is their secret?

Charisma starts with connection.

Charisma starts with connection. Making really deep and powerful connections with people you meet is the foundation of charisma. No connection equals no charisma.

How do you connect with people on a deep level? How do you make that person feel like he or she matters, that he or she is the only person in the room?

How do you develop charisma?

Remind yourself that:

There's no place else I'd rather be.
There's no one else I want to see.

Then listen the podcast by checking out iTunes and looking for the Danger and Play "Charisma and Connection."

Developing charisma will give you the game of an alpha male.

Women don't want to feel like you're rushing the process. Men become too preoccupied with this question, "How do I get her to go home?"

When men obsess over the next move, we become distracted and are no longer in the present moment. Women sense this, hence why we so often seem to miss out on what felt like a sure thing.

However, K Milli correctly notes that charisma for life is different from charisma for meeting women.

That is, the charisma that may makes you connect with others can in some ways hurt your connections with women. This is especially true of the diseased women that we often encounter in the Western world; that is, women who view men who want to make a genuine connection with them as being weak and lacking options.

Works cited:

- What Everybody is Saying
- Eye Contact Game
- Active Meditation and Getting in the Moment
- How to Move and Live with Purpose
- Everything is Connected
- Danger & Play on SoundCloud; Danger & Play on iTunes

How to Make Better Eye Contact

What color are your barista's eyes? You probably do not make eye contact with people, and it's costing you opportunities at your job and with women.

Making eye contact will teach you a lot about yourself and about others.

What a girl's eye contact says about her first impression of you.

If a girl looks down to the ground, she views herself as <u>having lower status</u> than you. If you meet a girl who looks down, do not act too cocky. She already feels insecure. Being too cocky will sabotage the exchange if you go on strong. Go direct with a simple, "Hi."

Girls who look to the side after making eye contact view you as an equal or an inferior. She is looking away (a dismissive tone) rather than down (which is submissive). Be cockier around girls who look at you sideways. Use indirect openings to catch their attention, and do not be afraid to tease them.

What if you look down rather than hold eye contact?

If *you* look down, it means you're submissive. If you look down after making eye contact with a woman, you have subconsciously told her that you're a worm. You've lost the game.

Girls seem to enjoy getting into staring contests. Hold the gaze and then smirk. If she smiles back, it means she is mirroring you reflexively. Call her over to you.

Learn the power stare.

If you want to fuck with someone's head, stare at her forehead. This is called the "power stare"; it's extremely effective on women you meet when you're out and it works in the workplace too.

Learn to look through people.

If you don't really care about your job and want to get out of the office, look down after your boss chews your ass. He will subconsciously process the eye movement as a sign of victory.

Sometimes you should lose the eye contact game.

If you care about your career, make eye contact and hold it. To avoid a power contest that you are sure to lose (but you don't want to submit either), divert your attention to something on your boss's desk. Then say, "I never noticed _____ about _____ before."

You can use a girl's eyes as a pick-up line.

The only time I compliment a woman is when I compliment her eyes. But don't just say, "You have purty eyes."

Say, "You have an intense gaze. Do men sometimes find that intimidating?" Then start talking about how infrequently people make eye contact. If you say something like, "People spend too much time looking at their iPhones," she is less likely to answer texts while you're talking to her.

Women are addicted to eye contact. If you frame the conversation by talking about her eyes, you will make a deeper connection with her.

All women like to believe that their eye color changes. This is especially true of girls with green eyes. If a woman has green eyes, say, "What color does your eyes change to in the sun?"

How to learn how to make better eye contact.

A simple way to learn how to make better eye contact is to practice on baristas, cashiers, and clerks. Imagine you are taking a quiz tomorrow. The quiz will ask you the eye color of ten people you interacted with the day before.

When buying coffee, ask yourself, "What color was the barista's eyes?"

You'll learn to hold eye contact long enough to find out the answer.

When you arrive at work, be prepared to answer the same question about your co-workers' eye colors.

If you can't say what color a person's eyes are, then you've failed the quiz.

Bonus tip: Your eyes will follow your chin. If you want to maintain good eye contact, keep your chin up.

Read more: *The Power of Eye Contact* (on Amazon).

Shame is the Game Killer

Most of us don't yet recognize—yet alone—admit a fact that defines our existence. Namely, we give complete strangers an incredible amount of power over our lives.

Imagine you're at a coffee shop by yourself when a cute girl walks by you. She sees you, smiles, and flicks her hair. It's obvious she wants you to approach. You're about to get up when... you stop.

There are other people around. What if your approach fails? These people will judge you. You'll be so ashamed.

What is the girl thinks you're a total loser? What if she thinks you're a creep?

Who cares what those people think?

Why do you care so much about the approval of complete strangers? If you forgot your wallet at home, how many people would even spot you $5 for a latte? If you were having a heart attack, do you think any of them would bother calling 911? They don't care about you. Why do you care so much about them?

A few years ago, as part of my path to self-development, I began eliminating shame from my consciousness. I started off small; for example, by wearing a shirt that was too flamboyant for a straight male. People would sneer. At first it bothered me. Then, as with all things in life, I acclimated. I began feeling nothing.

I'd make more approaches of women on buses and subways. People would often gawk or eavesdrop. Some seemed downright happy when I didn't get the girl's number. Yet consider what sort of boring life a hater must lead. I'm the most interesting thing that happens to most people. How pathetic.

Life is progressive resistance. In the gym you add more weight to the bar, and in life, you add challenges until you hurt. Adaptation requires overload.

The other night I went out in cowboy boots, a leather jacket with a fringe, and a cowboy hat. The guys in front of the bar were checking IDs. They flagged me and my crew right through, assuming that I was a celebrity. Girls were all over me.

Most guys would have feel like a complete tool wearing my outfit. Yet I felt normal. Relaxed. Comfortable. I felt no shame.

The only people whose opinions should matter are those who are there for you. I have a core group of friends. They are people I have been loyal to, and who have helped me in my own time of need. If they disapprove of something I'm doing, then I'll listen. I may disagree and continue doing it. But I'll feel something when they speak.

Complete strangers? Who cares? What they think or feel shouldn't prevent you from approaching a girl. Eliminate shame, and you will have eliminated the single biggest game killer.

Go for the Neck

One of the biggest mistakes guys make is going for the kiss too soon. A woman is on guard for a kiss attempt, which is why women often move their lips away from yours when you go for the kiss prematurely.

When a woman moves her lips away from you, too many guys kiss her on the cheek. There is a much better approach.

As she turns away, brush her hair aside, revealing her neck. Take a quick nibble on the side of her neck, look back up at her in the eyes, smirk, and then go back to dancing or talking at the bar. Do not go for a kiss immediately after nibbling on her neck. Wait a few minutes.

Women give up their neck surprisingly easy. Partially this is due to "vampiremania," with grown adult women obsessing over childhood vampires. Partially this is because few guys actually go for their neck. Women simply aren't prepared for the move.

Most women are also unaware how a gentle bite on their neck arouses them. The neck is a bona fide erogenous zone. If you nibble on her neck correctly, you'll notice goosebumps on her arms. Endorphins will be released, and blood flow to her vagina will increase.

I spend a lot of time on a woman's neck. Only after she is comfortable with my neck bites do I even try kissing her. I can get a woman far more turned on with "neck play" than kissing, and I only kiss her because kissing is a universal sign of intimacy. Otherwise, I'd stick to the neck.

Once I eventually kiss her, it's an immediate (and hot) make-out session. The woman is highly aroused.

Moreover, a bite on the neck is a subtle dominance play. Anyone who has observed dogs can see that smaller dogs roll over and reveal their necks to the larger dogs. Unconsciously, by revealing her neck, she has already allowed herself to be submissive to you.

Although women often make me delay kissing them, I can usually start playing with a girl's neck within 30 minutes of meeting her.

One does not need to wait to be rejected from a kiss before nibbling on the neck. I always find excuses to play with her neck. I'll pull her closely to me to "whisper" something in her ear. Then I will take a gentle bite on her neck, smirk, and continue the conversation.

When nibbling on her neck, the only requirement is to not overdo it at first. Women fear hickeys, and once they realize you're not making sloppy sucking noises or biting her, she will let you have her way with you.

Neck play is foreplay you can do in public, and within two hours—once you're good at it—you will be fucking her.

What is Lifestyle Game?

I'm not sure how others use the term "lifestyle game," and I don't really care. To me, lifestyle game means creating a life for yourself that you allow worthy girls into.

That is, you don't pretend to be someone else in order to meet a girl. Instead, you have an actual sense of self and a well-defined lifestyle that you allow suitable women to share with you.

I'll give you a recent example.

My friend was digging a chick. The only debate is whether she's an 8.5 or 9. Whatever the case, this is the kind of girl other men obsess over.

This chick is now totally in love with my boy. She experienced the lifestyle, and now she doesn't want to leave. In fact, she's terrified of being removed from the lifestyle.

On Friday, she came over for grilled rib eye, artichokes (steamed, then grilled), steamed vegetables, and mochi. She drank complex wine. We went out to a cool club, had some bottles of vodka, and woke up. Then we had an elegant brunch. Afterwards, we strolled through the city, attending a street fair. Later, we stopped for espresso.

We did nothing out of the ordinary for this new girl.

Whether or not she came over, we'd have grilled thick cuts of prime steak. We'd have gone out to a cool club. We'd have had brunch, and we'd have done some sort of cool activity. Nothing changed for her.

Now, look at how the game changes. One, there's no way to screw up your game, since you're not running game. You are simply doing what you always do. Your girl is coming over? Cool, I'll make an extra plate.

Second, you create a lifestyle so awesome that a woman doesn't want to leave it. If you're a man who hits the weight room, likes to go out once a week, drinks fine wine, and eats good food, you're going to find a lot of women willing to audition.

Third, you always have the lifestyle. Whether or not a chick comes over on Friday, I'm grilling steak and asparagus. I'll be opening a bottle of wine. When your lifestyle as a man is awesome, you often view women as an unwelcome intrusion. Do I even want to invite a girl over?

When you hold yourself to high standards, you become picky, which women immediately sense. Often when I go out, I think, "All of these women are boring. I don't want to share my steaks and wine with them. Can I imagine them on the couch, talking to my roommate? They will bore him, and they may even steal some artwork. I'm not going to even talk to them." Suddenly women are asking me why I'm "not having a good time." They sense my superiority complex, and are horny to find out what's behind it.

Fourth, what do you suppose it does for the girl's princess complex when she realizes that she is walking into your lifestyle?

We don't roll out the red carpet for them. We roll it out for ourselves.

If she's lucky, she gets to walk down it with us.

Once you create the best version of yourself, you'll find yourself rejecting more women than ever.

The Five Stages of Game Consciousness

I don't read many websites about picking up women, because they are at the lower levels of consciousness. I don't say this as a way to hate, because being at a lower level is necessary if one is to reach higher levels. I was once at a lower level, too.

How is this lower level manifested? It manifests in the anger stages under the Kübler-Ross/Five Stages of Grief model.

"The Kübler-Ross model, or the five stages of grief, is a series of emotional stages experienced when faced with impending death or death of someone. The five stages are denial, anger, bargaining, depression and acceptance."

Denial is where 90% of American men are. These are the beta males who deny the truth about women. When they are rejected and abused by American women, the beta makes excuses. "She only behaved that way because of..."

Men living in denial use terms like "douchebag" and "dudebro" to refer to men who are successful with women. The man living in denial simply has no concept of what women want.

Anger is where 90% of PUAs and others who write about women are. The angry tone is evident in the writing.

Once guys leave the denial phase, they are outraged at the abuse women expect these men to take and the levels of entitlement possessed by the most mediocre of women.

These men are obsessed with unfairness and double standards. Instead of coolly exploiting the system, they vent and rage.

Bargaining is a level of consciousness few men reach, and yet it's only a middle-tier level of awareness. The "bargaining man" agrees that women are problematic, but claims the modern American woman will change if he only runs strong relationship game. "My game is tight, so my girl won't pull the stunts she pulls on other guys." He is always making deals with women rather than showing them the door.

Depression hits when a man realizes that everything he learned about women was a lie. Maybe he finds out she is searching for ex-boyfriends on Facebook.

Once you understand women, it becomes harder to deal with them. Parents avoid petulant children, and a high-level man starts avoiding the women-children that comprise the vast majority of American females. The "depressed man" asks: "Why bother?"

Acceptance is where a man accepts women as they are, but on his own terms. The "accepting man" knows American women are incorrigible, while also realizing he himself enjoys sex and occasional female companionship. He gets what he wants, but does not believe he will change the fundamental nature of broken woman. He lives a life of freedom.

Stop being negative and start being alpha.

Friends and Family

Should You Disown Your Family?

One of the most commonly asked questions on game forums goes something like this:

"How can I explain what I am doing to my family? My mom tells me I should settle down with a good girl. My dad thinks my lifestyle is immoral. My brothers and sisters judge me. What can I do?"

The short answer is that you don't explain shit. Unless someone is living the life you want to live, why are you even listening to them?

People don't like how you are living? What have they accomplished? What qualifies them to tell you anything about life?

Oh, because they are family?

So what? My brother is a loser who just got out of prison for shooting his meth dealer. I haven't talked to him in a decade. Why would I associate with such a scumbag? Because he's family?

Guess what, you are only responsible for your own choices. Did you choose your family?

I would love having a cool younger brother. It would be badass to hit the gym with a guy with whom I had 30+ years of shared history. It'd be awesome to go into business together. It'd be great to run game.

But I didn't get to choose my brother. Instead of having a legit dude who wanted to go places, I ended up with a real shitbagger. Oh well.

Your mom doesn't like how you live? Well, that's her problem, not yours, because it's your life, not hers.

Why does your mom—who should love you unconditionally—care more about some random girl whose finger you'd put a ring on than about you?

Is your mom more loyal to her gender than to her own son? If that's the case, you need to tell mom to drop the subject or else you're hanging up the phone.

Your dad doesn't like your lifestyle? Again, that's his problem. You dad was foolish enough to marry your mom, after all. That's proof enough he's unqualified to talk about the game.

You didn't ask to be born. You don't owe your parents anything. Your parents were motivated by evolutionary forces to procreate. They selfishly choose to have you. You can selfishly decide whether or not to keep them.

If you want to become a man, you will need to reject the losers. That includes your family.

Some may read this post and think I have a horrible relationship with my family. Those people (haters) would be wrong.

I have a great relationship with my father. I love him and will always be there for him.

I worship my grandmother. She was a matriarch who kept our family together when times were tough and she raised good sons.

But I love my family based on their merits and not out of some Hallmark card sentimentality.

If your family is holding you back, cut the cord and begin living life as a man.

Building Your Crew

It was my junior year in high school. Like most nights, I was at a friend's house smoking weed.

After smoking some especially good weed, time stopped. I had a moment of clarity.

I looked around the trailer. "This is what's to become of me?"

My friends would call. I wouldn't call them back. I summarily ended relationships with five of my closest friends.

I was too young to realize it, but I had stumbled upon a major pillar of life success.

"You are the average of the five people you spend the most time with." – Jim Rohn

Consider, for example, this study on fat people:

"Wondering why your waistline is expanding? Have a look at those of your friends. Your close friends can influence your weight even more than genes or your family members, according to new research appearing in the July 26 issue of The New England Journal of Medicine. The study's authors suggest that obesity isn't just spreading; rather, it may be contagious between people, like a common cold."

That may seem abstractly shocking. How could having fat friends make me fat? They don't peer pressure me into eating.

"We are what we do. We are not what we think, or what we feel, or what we say, we are what we do." – Gordon Livingston

A person didn't just become fat by the waving of some magician's wand. The fat person chose to be fat. He made bad choice after bad choice. The person is fat because of what he does.

Your four fat friends call you to go out to eat, and you agree. The fat guys are not going to hit up a sushi joint. They're going to want to go to Marconi Grill or Cheesecake Factory.

Because you've been conditioned to be polite, you're going to eat at a shit restaurant with these people. Because of the framing and anchoring cognitive biases, your food choice will be based on what your fat friend orders. "I'll eat some spinach and artichoke dip, as that's not nearly as bad as the appetizer platter he ordered."

Suddenly your own waistline has swelled. You might not be as fat as your four friends, but they have made you fatter.

The opposite is true. If your friends are fit, you'll be fit, too. On a Saturday afternoon, your friends will be at the gym and then eating light meals. If you want to hang with them, you're going to go where they want to go.

Suddenly, you're in better shape.

If you're out with guys who approach women, you're going to approach more women. Even if you don't approach as often as your friends, you'll still have access to more women than you would if your guys were cowardly beta bitches who tremor at the sight of a beautiful woman. Your average notch count will increase, simply by virtue of hanging out with players.

My table scraps are better than most men's meals.

Having a legit crew will raise you up. The problem with most men is that they refuse to break up with shitty friends. Guys will complain that their friends are mooching, or not buying drinks, or hiding out when the check arrives.

A friendship is a garden. You must water the flowers and pull out the weeds.

If you hang out with losers, you will become a loser. If you hang out with winners, you will become a winner.

If I had stayed in that house smoking weed, I'd be stuck working some shit job in a shit downtown, married to some shit cow and raising some shit kids.

I decided to "raise my average."

As with most decisions, it's one we must reaffirm often. I always tell myself, "Raise your average." If a guy is slowing my roll, he's out.

But don't just look at your friends. Look in a mirror.

Raising your average means stepping up your own game. Success is a virtuous circle. The tighter your game is, the tighter your friends' game will be.

Everyone will bring everyone up. Or everyone will bring everyone down:

"When a single crab is put into a lidless bucket, they surely can and will escape. However, when more than one share a bucket, none can get out. If one crab elevates themself above all, the others will grab this crab and drag 'em back down to share the mutual fate of the rest of the group."

Get away from people who will bring you down. Get them out of your life, and no situation in life will seem inescapable.

How to Find Legit Friends: The Ten-Year Test

Dear *Danger & Play:*

Most guys my age are really lame. You have written somewhat abstractly about the important of "building your crew," but never gave any practical tips on how to do so. What is your advice?

Someone could write a treatise about friendship, and I encourage you to read the *Nicomachean Ethics*. I've distilled all of the writing down to one heuristic. Like all heuristics—which are just thinking shortcuts—this rule is not a hundred percent accurate. There are exceptions. NAMALT. This rule will serve you right more often than it will steer you wrong.

Does he have friendships dating back at least ten years?

Why is this so important?

I hate to break it to you, but we are all diseased. 2Wycked is one of my favorite manosphere bloggers and he writes about narcissism. Yet he seems to miss the joke: he's every bit as narcissistic as those he observes.

That's not a dig at him. It's simply a recognition of reality: a man cannot escape his culture. We all suffer from varying degrees of sociopathy, narcissism, and alienation.

I, for example, am not particularly narcissistic. But you could tell me that your mom died and I wouldn't feel anything. It takes a lot for me to register anything approaching emotional pain. (One exception: the Sarah McLachlan animal cruelty video.)

My friends tend to be highly narcissistic and needy. They need to be "fed," as I like to put it.

Yet my friends and I are all self-aware. We know we are sick, we're okay with it, and we form symbiotic relationships based on our respective psychopathologies.

The relationships work because I'm not needy. I don't need to be fed, thus we're not competing for attention/ego feeding. In public, they can go seek out attention and I just do my own thing.

Men who do not realize they are sick are users and parasites. They cannot have functional relationships because they lack the self-awareness to understand that they are takers. They do not "even the ledger."

Someone who doesn't have meaningful friendships dating back ten years (for you younger guys, maybe it should be the Five-Year Rule) has blown everyone out. What do I mean by *blown out?*

We all know the guy who shows up at the bar and never buys the first round. Using a form of game theory, he optimizes his free drinks by always letting someone else buy the first round. If you buy the last round, you aren't immediately spotted as a cheat because you did buy a round.

Yet look at a game involving 3 men and 5 drinks.

- A: Buys 1st round
- B: Buys 2nd round
- C: Buys 3rd round
- A: Buys 4th round (his second round)
- B: Buys 5th round (his second round)
- C: [Everyone goes home; avoids buying second round]

There's always that one guy who puts himself in C's position, right? We all know that guy who is never the designated driver. He never buys the first round. He never greases the door guy. He never wants to do something that everyone else wants to do. He always looks out for himself, foolishly unable to recognize that it's better to be long-term greedy than to skim off the top in the short term.

Those freeloaders and mooches can get away with that for a while, but eventually your brain picks up on it. We have evolved to play tit-for-tat:

"Tit for tat is an English saying meaning 'equivalent retaliation.' It is also a highly effective strategy in game theory for the iterated prisoner's dilemma. The strategy was first introduced by Anatol Rapoport in Robert Axelrod's two tournaments, held around 1980. Notably, it was (on both occasions) both the simplest strategy and the most successful.

"An agent using this strategy will first cooperate, then subsequently replicate an opponent's previous action. If the opponent previously was cooperative, the agent is cooperative. If not, the agent is not. This is similar to superrationality and reciprocal altruism in biology."

Much of this is subconscious. Men don't usually do a full accounting of the meal when the check comes, unlike women. We are "rough justice" animals. Sure, maybe one guy had a glass of wine while you drank water, but why not split the check 50-50 anyway? Or why don't I just grab it this time and you can grab it next time?

Who keeps track of who bought the last round? We don't consciously note it.

When some guy is always in position C, you start resenting the guy, even if it's only subconsciously. You don't return his calls and he falls off the shelf.

The guy who can't name friends he has had for several years has been person "C" in every relationship.

So my advice is this: look for men who have several long-lasting relationships. Even if the person is a nut, he at least understands how to even a ledger. He's not going to skip out on checks, use you for your cash, try banging your girlfriend, or pull any of the other bullshit that 90 percent of modern guys try pulling.

And if you do not have friendships going back decades, perhaps it is not other men who are lame. Perhaps the problem is you.

Do You Hide Who You Are?

A reader writes in:

"One of the hardest things about taking the red pill is that I feel like I can't be myself at work and around friends and family. I have to bite my lip and keep quiet. How do you handle it?"

This is a fairly common concern. The answer has two components: psychological and practical.

You are afraid of being yourself because you fear rejection. You are afraid that your family and friends will forsake you. You're trying to rationalize it as something else, but that's ultimately what's going on.

Therefore, you need to get your mind right. Work on your "inner game" or "frame" or whatever you want to call it. If you fear rejection, your inner game is weak because it means you rely on other people to validate your identity.

Your concern reminded me of a quote about work from Fight Club:

"We buy things we don't need with money we don't have to impress people we don't like."

You say things you don't mean to impress people you don't like.

Be honest. Do you like your blue pill friends and relatives? Perhaps I'm guilty of projection, but I hate blue pill people.

I view blue pill people with contempt. If you're a compassionate person, maybe you pity rather than hate them.

Do you even like these people?

Chances are that you do not. What do you have to lose by being yourself? You have nothing to lose but losers, parasites, leeches, and deadweight.

Be yourself. If your views offend them, wish them well on their journey and part ways. **This includes your family**.

91

If you do not like these people, why would you fear their rejection? Your fear is irrational, because you fear mice when you aspire to be a lion.

Now you might say that you have to bite your lip at work due to political correctness and HR concerns. If that's true, I would ask you something:

Are you going to be a CEO of a Fortune 500 company?

If you're not going to be a CEO, why care if you can get a shit job at some corporation? I could never be hired at Coca-Cola, Pepsi, or State Farm. Some woman in HR would Google my name (there is nothing I've said at this blog that I haven't said in real life or under my real name) and that'd be the end of my job search.

You know what? I don't give a shit, because sitting in a cubicle and living in fear of the fatties and losers in HR would be a version of hell.

I haven't had a W-2 in over 11 years. I've been on my own, running my own business for over a decade. There's no reason you need to work for some shit company.

As with your fear of rejection, your fear of being *persona non grata* to some shit corporation is irrational.

I have incredibly rich and successful friends and business associates. Many of them think I am a lazy bum and would love to have me working with them. Finding a job would be as easy as making a phone call. This is true even though *I do not have a résumé*.

Many men agree with what I write and say in real life. The most successful a man is, the more likely he will agree with my message.

It's only the weak and pathetic who disagree with me. Why do you want to work and associate with the weak? Is it worth swimming in vomit for the chance that you might someday earn six figures?

What does it profit a man, if he gains the money to shop at Ikea and wear khaki pants, and lose his soul?

It takes a while to have the "inner game" to just be true to who you are and recognize that many will reject you. At first, the rejection may sting. We probably evolved to fear rejection because we used to live in close knit communities of 150 or so people.

In a small community, rejection could mean the difference between life and death. Piss off a tribe elder and suddenly you'll have a "hunting accident," or be forbidden from marrying his daughter.

Nowadays, rejection doesn't mean anything. Unlike our primitive ancestors, we are not born into a community. We have the power to create our own communities.

When you stop lying about who you are, you will actually have legitimate friendships and business relationships. The people in your life will be there when you need them to be, and you will gladly be there for them when they need you.

In conclusion:

Stop pretending to be something you're not in order to win the approval of people you don't like.

Business and Career Success

Make Big Moves

He was a mid-level manager who paid his dues working at various blue-chip companies. Because his reputation was sterling, my friend called him in for an interview at his company: a young start-up with a potentially huge upside.

Everyone liked the manager. He was given the standard offer: a significant pay cut with a nice slice of equity. He would earn less but be a part owner in the company.

"I talked it over with my wife. We can't afford to take a 20 percent pay cut. It's too risky."

My friend begged him to reconsider. "You will fit in well at the company. The stock offer is generous. It's a chance for you to potentially get rich."

"My wife said we can't swing it."

Everyone was sorry to hear the manager's answer. Three months later, the stock split. This wasn't a total surprise, as the stock had split twice before. The company brutalized its employees. But employees were true owners. To get paid as an owner, you had better be prepared to work like one.

The manager's shares had quadrupled in value. At last check, his shares would have been worth $1,044,450. After taxes. Thirty-five years old. One-million dollars. Cash. Money in the bank.

The manger could blame his wife, the wind, or his God. He could tell himself that the grapes on the highest branches are the least sweet.

While he sings himself childish lullabies to help him sleep at night, others are deciding where to take their next vacation. Many are taking permanent vacations, retiring from work or taking on easier jobs with lower salaries and collecting yield.

In this lifetime, a man gets one or two chances to make a big move. You'll know it's time to make your move when the decision hurts.

If the manager had left his stable job, he'd have taken a pay cut. He'd have to had cut costs substantially. His wife would have nagged him. Whenever they couldn't pay a bill or eat out or pay for a babysitter, she'd have reminded him how much more money he'd have made at his old job.

If he had been willing to endure the pain of yesterday, today he'd be rich.

When it's time, make your move.

Finding Your Force: Leverage or Momentum? Part 1

There are two primary forces within the universe and each of us taps into the energy in a different way. Although there is overlap between the two forces, all of us tend towards one or the other. We either use leverage or momentum to accomplish our goals.

It's important to know which "type" you are because each approach has pros and cons. A momentum type, for example, tends to make things happen. But a momentum type also stumbles into some traps, as the desire to keep moving somewhere often leads down him blind alleys.

A leverage type is efficient and rarely wastes energy. They move with determination. Yet their cautious nature often causes them to miss out on opportunities.

Are you a leverage or a momentum type? Take this test to find out.

Before taking the personality inventory, keep in mind that most people are a little bit of both. The idea is to find which type you tend towards.

Which most or best describes you?

(Check all that apply.)

1. ✓ I'm always in a hurry to get things done.
2. ✓ When I get something done, I want to move onto something else.
3. ✓ When I haven't been productive, it's hard for me to get moving.

4. __ ✓ I've rushed into some decisions (investment, personal etc.) that I later regretted.

5. __ ✓ People think I'm intense and angry.

6. ___ I think that other people are too spazzy and frenzied. They should chill out.

7. ___ You should wait for the "right place, right time" before making a move.

8. ___ I like to take my time to deliberate and have every piece of information before making a decision.

9. ___ I have missed out on some good opportunities in my life because I didn't act quickly enough.

10. ___ People think I'm too chill and sometimes view me as "checked out."

If you checked more boxes in Questions 1-5, you're a momentum type. If you checked more boxes in Questions 6-10, then you're a leverage type.

The pros and cons of momentum and leverage types.
Momentum Types

Some people need momentum to get things done. Move. Smash. Keep moving. I am a momentum type.

Pros: We get things done quickly. We are decisive, creative, and audacious.

Cons: Because we either "move or die," we fall into traps and take on undue risk. When we lose momentum, we have negative momentum. As Newtown observed, "An object at rest stays at rest, and an object in motion stays in motion."

Leverage Types

They wait for the right time to move with maximum efficiency. My boy Nic is a leverage type.

"Give me a place to stand on, and I will move the Earth." – Archimedes.

Pros: They don't waste energy. They are efficient. When they move, their moves count.

Cons: They can be indecisive. They miss out on opportunities waiting for the perfect time to act. Yet as anyone who has lived for a few decades has learned, there is often no perfect time to move.

Which type are you?

In the next installment of the series, I'll talk more about the two different types. I'll even discuss how momentum and leverage types can work together to form amazing partnerships.

Which type are you: a momentum type or a leverage type?

Leverage and Momentum: Part 2, How You Work

How Leverage Types Work

"Give me a stick long enough and a pivot and I shall move the world," the crafty Greek physicist Archimedes observed. Although Archimedes did not discover the lever, he did refine and explain the principles behind leverage.

The leverage type is smart and analytical. They do not waste too many movements. Like Archimedes, leverage types say, "Give me a place to stand on, and I will move the Earth."

The leverage type takes in all available information and then makes one or two really smart, efficient moves that lead to great results. Careful and deliberative is how to describe a leverage type, with the emphasis on careful.

Warren Buffett is the archetype of the leverage type. His investment strategy embodies the leverage type of thinking. In a speech on investing years ago, he said that most investors should only be allowed to make 20 trades over the course of their investing life.

Buffett theorized that most people trade in and out of the stock market far too often. (There's even an investing strategy called *momentum investing*.) This causes the vast majority of investors to "buy high and sell low." If you could only make 20 trades in the course of your life, you'd be careful to only make the right trades, wouldn't you?

He told students at the University of Georgia (fast forward to 31:05 in the video, although the entire video is worth watching):

"You would be better off if when you got out of school, you got a punch card with 20 punches. Every financial decision you made, you

100

used up a punch. You'd get very rich because you'd think through each one very hard."

https://www.youtube.com/watch?v=2a9Lx9J8uSs

The pitfall of being a leverage type is that they are often too risk-averse. "Big opportunities in life have to be seized." Make big moves.

In the same speech to students at the University of Georgia, Buffett himself noted that he missed out on some big opportunities. "I've cost Berkshire at least $5 billion by sucking my thumb," he told the audience.

How Momentum Types Work

Momentum types move with swiftness, boldness, and audacity. This allows them to achieve great things because they go where angels fear to tread.

General George S. Patton is an outstanding example of a momentum type. As Patton remarked, "Audacity, audacity, always audacity!" Patton ran through Germany and caused havoc and we wouldn't have been in the Cold War with the Soviet Union if Patton had been allowed to keep moving.

The problem with momentum types is that they assume too much risk and often speak and act too freely. Patton lost a command after he smacked a soldier who claimed to suffer from "battle fatigue" (what we now know to be PTSD).

He also spoke too openly about the Russians, observing:

"The Russians are Mongols. They are Slavs and a lot of them used to be ruled by ancient Byzantium. From Genghis Khan to Stalin. they have not changed. They never will and we will never learn, at least, not until it is too late."

Even though political correctness wasn't the dominant force, Patton lost his position for speaking out openly against what was then an "ally" of the United States.

No approach is right.

A leverage and momentum type can each accomplish great things. Neither approach is right or wrong. However, each type must have some self-awareness and realize where his strength and weaknesses lie. "First, know thyself."

If you're a leverage type, are you sitting behind a desk waiting for that perfect type to quit your job to start your own business?

If you're a momentum type, are you too frantically moving when you should instead pause, reflect, and strategize before making a major decision?

Leverage or Momentum: Part 3, Partnerships

As leverage and momentum types have different strengths and weaknesses, you need to think long and hard before forming a business partnership. (Indeed, one of the biggest business mistakes men make is partnering up with a friend just because you are friends, though that's a subject for another post.)

Momentum-Momentum Partnerships

Two momentum types working together had better be careful. They won't see each other's blind sides. Everything will be rush-rush-rush and no one will ever put on the breaks. Two momentum types can achieve great success, but they are just as likely to blow up the business by taking on too much risk, always doing business deals, and taking action simply for the sake of doing something.

Leverage-Leverage Partnerships

Two leverage types who work together will waste a lot time and pass on many profitable opportunities. They won't make anything happen. They'll suck on their thumbs all day.

Of course that's not always true. But if you are careful and deliberative, you had better ensure that your partner isn't quite as careful and deliberate as you are.

The Momentum-Leverage Partnership

Synergy is the most overused, cliché, dumb word in the corporate lexicon. Yet here the word actually applies. When a leverage and momentum type work together, the sum is greater than the parts.

How To Work Together

1. Recognize that conflict is inevitable.

Because of your different ways of viewing the world, a leverage type will think a momentum type is being too brash and spazzy. A momentum type will think that a leverage type is taking too long.

That's fine. Conflict is okay among men. Just don't take things personally or be a little girl about it.

2. You're not allowed to judge.

If you are working with someone of genuine accomplishment, you can't judge. You are not right. Your type is not right. The other person's type is not right.

Both types can accomplish great things.

So shut up and stop getting indignant when someone disagrees with you.

3. Focus on what matters.

You are working together towards a common goal. When conflict happens, remind yourself of the goal you and your partner are working towards.

Everything is secondary to your goals.

Your feelings are hurt? You didn't like the email? Wah. Doesn't matter. As long as the goals are accomplished, you are winning.

4. Learn from the other type.

If you're a momentum type, your brashness and boldness creates opportunity but also leads to costly mistakes.

If you're a leverage type, your patience mitigates risk and can help protect you from harm. But life is risk and the more (intelligent) risk you take on, the greater your rewards.

Look at what the other person is doing, almost like you're a psychologist. Ask yourself why the person is doing what he's doing.

View it from an optimistic angle. "Oh, he isn't being lazy. He just thinks now is too soon to move," the momentum type might say of the leverage type.

"He's right, there is no optimal time to move. We need to create an opportunity that doesn't already exist," the leverage type might say of the momentum type.

5. Meet in the middle.

Conflict is best understood in the Hegelian sense. Leverage is thesis. Momentum is antithesis.

Once you resolve the conflict, the synthesis will be better than either of you.

Make big, bold moves. Smash things, momentum types.

But why swing a an axe when you can split a log much easier by putting a split
into it?

What's Your Take?

What type do you identify with? What are your biggest strengths and weaknesses resulting from your type?

Go Full Gorilla

Jonah Hill was a politically correct actor who was stalked by the paparazzi. In a moment of weakness, he used the word "faggot." He went on TV to cry.

Dr. Matt Taylor was a good little boy who followed all of the rules. He earned a Ph.D. in astrophysics and eventually landed a satellite on a comet moving 150,000 miles per hour.

Dr. Matt Taylor is literally a rocket scientist:

*"Matt Taylor was born in London, gained his undergraduate Physics degree at the University of Liverpool, and a PhD from Imperial College London. His career has focused on the space plasma measurements, working in Europe and the US on the four spacecraft ESA Cluster mission, leading to a post at ESA which started in 2005 working as the project scientist for Cluster and the ESA-China Double star mission. His studies have focused on energetic particle dynamics in near-Earth space and in the interaction of the Sun's solar wind with the Earth's magnetic field, particularly focusing on how boundary layer interactions evolve, **leading to 70 first or co-authored papers**. Most recently he was appointed the Project Scientist on the Rosetta mission."*

Dr. Matt Taylor was even a bit of a hipster, with full arm sleeve tattoos. If you had asked him about *Danger & Play* two weeks ago, he'd probably have called my site offensive.

Men like Matt Taylor don't need Danger & Play. They are better than we are. They are accepted by mainstream society.

What was Dr. Matt Taylor's reward for being a good little slave?

After landing a satellite on a moving comet somewhere far away in outer space, he gave a press conference. During that press conference he—showing his street cred as a hipster—donned a garish bowling shirt.

("We landed on a moving comet!" – Dr. Matt Taylor after winning the Superbowl of science.)

There was immediate outcry. Forget this man's grand achievement. His shirt had women on it. How offensive!

An online hate mob formed and Dr. Taylor began receiving harassment and death threats from radical feminists and social justice warriors (SJWs).

Rather than stand up and rebel against his slave masters, Dr. Matt backed down. He was not trained in the Gorilla Mindset ways.

Dr. Matt Taylor went on television to give a tearful apology. He cried on television, supplicating before his slave masters.

Now do you see why I am the way I am?

I am a legit legal scholar with publications to my name. My legal writing has been cited in federal court opinions. I am recognized by lawyers as an expert on constitutional law and civil rights litigation.

But unless I bow down to the SJWs (which includes sex offenders and other social deviants), I will always be under attack. I'll always be a "bad" person.

Only complete and total surrender of your soul will placate the SJWs who went after Matt Taylor.

That's not going to happen. Yes, I am all the SJWs hate. I embrace the hate and love it. I went full gorilla!

Go full gorilla.
(Or as Ice-T says, "Fuck it!")

Be who you are: without apologies or remorse or regrets. It is your life, not theirs.

Cast aside any aspirations of mainstream acceptance, unless you're willing to crawl on your knees before *Gawker*.

Gawker and the SJWs will come after you. It's only a matter of time.

But they can't come after you if, like me, you laugh in their pathetic faces and punch them in the nose when they assault you. *Gawker* writers have been instructed to not write about me, because I so humiliated Sam Biddle that he needed a 30-day leave of absence to collect himself.

Go full gorilla.

What is stopping you from being you?

Three Ways a Tony Robbins Seminar Changed Danger & Play

About one year ago I attended Unleash the Power Within (UPW) in Los Angeles. A friend of mine had always wanted to attend one and we were able to get in for half off the list price (buy one get one free). Otherwise I would not have gone, and that would have been a terrible mistake.

For some, change comes fast. I didn't attend UPW because I was looking for my messiah or looking for answers to major questions in my life. Any change was going to be gradual.

I went in with an open mind and to address a couple of issues.

My biggest life problem at the time was being a victim of my success. I had made enough smart moves in my 20s that I lacked motivation in my 30s. I didn't have any problems. No worries with money. No worries with women. Everything was great.

When everything is going well, you can lose that hunger. In a way it's better to fight to become a champion than to become the champion. Champs get fat and lazy. You stop growing as a man.

I took three major points from the seminar and have made some lasting changes.

1. I am much more aware of and in control of my state.

I'm much more conscious of state control. Before UPW I was more likely to be ruled by my moods. If I didn't feel like doing something, I wouldn't do it. After all, having money means you don't have to do anything you don't want to do.

I realized that letting my moods ruled me was beta. How could I just passively accept moods? Wouldn't the right approach be to change my state?

Now do things that I'm not in the "mood" to do. Lately my sleep quality has been absolute garbage. I didn't feel like writing today or yesterday or the day before or the week before that.

Yet I've written more words and done more podcasts in the past week than I had in any week of 2013. If fact, my biggest problem now is that there are too many ebook, blog post, and podcast ideas.

When I don't feel like doing something, instead of letting the feeling rule me I change my state. It has changed my life.

2. Limiting beliefs and introversion.

I get a lot of emails from readers. I always felt bad that guys would reach out to me and I'd ignore them. I'd tell myself, "Well, I'm introverted. Talking to people wears me down. Sorry but I gotta do what I gotta do."

I started treating my introversion as a limiting belief. (A limiting belief if *something you tell yourself* about the world that is not true.)

Although I am still naturally introverted, I can interact with far more people than ever before without being worn out. I still need my alone time, but my ability to engage with others has at least doubled.

The next time you don't want to do something, ask if it's because you believe you're incapable of doing it. Change your state to one of certainty and attack that limiting belief.

3. I have been finding my motivation.

When you're broke or struggling with meeting women, motivation is easy to find. Get paid and get laid are the two most primal drives of mankind.

Although far from rich, I had attained the perfect amount of money. To paraphrase Warren Buffett, "The perfect amount of money is enough money to feel like you could do anything, but not so much that you could do nothing."

Money was initially my highest priority because I grew up poor. I never traveled more than an hour away from home because the car might not start and we'd be stranded. We'd run out of soap and I'd have to use dishwashing soap like Dawn to bathe in. Once my teacher sent me to the school bathroom to wash up because my elbows were caked with soot.

Now I can afford organic soaps from Whole Foods. I'm a simple man with simple needs. Some keep score with money. That's not my game. Money simply doesn't motivate me. You guys can make all the money and I'll live vicariously through you. Just invite me to a yacht party every now and then, cool?

What's my motivation? To find your motivation you need to look at your needs.

Tony Robbins claims there are Six Human Needs:

1.   **Certainty**: assurance you can avoid pain and gain pleasure

2.   **Uncertainty/Variety**: the need for the unknown, change, new stimuli

3.   **Significance**: feeling unique, important, special or needed

4.   **Connection/Love**: a strong feeling of closeness or union with someone or something

5.   **Growth**: an expansion of capacity, capability or understanding

6.   **Contribution**: a sense of service and focus on helping, giving to and supporting others

I had certainty and variety and significance and connection and growth. What was missing? Contribution. I found the focus Danger & Play needed.

Contribution and Danger & Play.

Instead of being "all things to all people," I decided to focus on who mattered to me. D&P is for a younger (or, as the TRT posts show, an older) version of me. Those are whom I would contribute to.

At one time I was a young guy who would have done whatever it took to succeed. I just didn't know what to do.

It took me sleepless nights, panic attacks, self-doubt, and a lack of certainty that I was on the right path. After much struggle I figured out life. Instead of keeping it to myself, I show what worked for me (while noting that what works for you might be something different).

By changing D&P's focus I actually turned off a lot of guys and lost traffic. Some whined my blog wasn't written for average people:

Some relatively decent advice, with a few gaps…but delivered in your usual douchebag frat-boy jock manner.

If you're looking to help the majority of men…you'd be better off presenting your information in a manner that the average person can relate to more easily.

I am not interested in helping the majority of men. I don't need to cast a wide net to draw in massive amounts of readers in order to fill my pockets with advertising dollars. D&P is written for a niche audience. It's for the 5% of people who will make it.

If someone posts a comment that I think is pathetic, I delete it. If someone wants to argue, they are banned. If someone doesn't "get it," then I say, "Good bye."

Danger & Play is for people who will do whatever it takes to succeed. We're not going to spend our time writing or speaking for people who want to complain that the price of success is too high.

Get on board with the mission – which is mastering *your* own life – or go be with the normal people.

3 Ways to Never Get Rich

Everyone wants to be rich, but that begs the question: What is rich? After all, you can't get rich if you don't know what rich is.

A recent email exchange with a reader illustrates the problem of getting rich.

<u>Reader</u>: *I write to you today as I would like to hear more about your opinion of the so called 'Law of Attraction,' particularly putting it in action on a daily basis.*

<u>Me</u>: Let's start off this way. What is it that you want to attract?

<u>Reader</u>: *Wealth. Shameless as it may well be, I'm in my twentiess, and I want to be rich now whilst I'm young to truly experience amazing things, not when I'm old.*

<u>Me</u>: What is wealth? What is rich? Why is being over 30 old?

<u>Reader</u>:

a) Wealth as in money, which opens doors;

b) Rich as in quality of life experience; and

c) Old as in incapable of fully enjoying the fruits of the world (as facilitated by money).

<u>Me</u>: What does that even mean?

The reader has been told his entire life he needs to get rich. Does he even known what the perfect day as a rich man would look like?

What is rich?

I've heard many people give their answer over the years. *The Millionaire Next Door* (Amazon) says you're rich when you have enough in savings to sustain your current lifestyle for teny years without working.

It seems more that everyone has a different definition of rich.

The best definition of rich I've ever heard comes from Naval Ravikant. In an interview some years ago, he said something that stuck with me.

The interviewer asked him about his fuck-you number. (It wasn't phrased *quite* like that.) In other words, how much more money would Ravikant need to make before he was done? His answer stuck with me.

"More money wouldn't change how I live my life."

That is rich.

Now some take issue with that definition. I brought up that definition the other day on Twitter.

A friend of mine said, "Mike, you have a BMW convertible. Of course more money would change how you live. You'd buy a Ferrari!"

I don't like talking about my net worth, because it's not relevant to my message. Some would be surprised to learn that I've done OK.

It is not sour grapes to say I have enough.

Yes, my lifestyle is humble. Many of you would view me as a simple man who wears old clothing. On any given day I am wearing one of several different Henleys from H&M that cost $9.95 each.

I do not appear to be successful or intelligent. If anything, I look like a gym rat.

More money would not change my daily routine. Money is not what I live for.

Does this mean I don't want more money? No. I am actively pursuing several different revenue streams (rivers, actually).

But my desire to earn more money is not out of some misguided effort to get rich. It is because making money *ethically* is a sure sign that you are delivering value and goodwill to the world.

Now that we know what it means to be rich, let's talk about those three ways to never get rich.

How to never get rich.

1. Don't appreciate what you have. If you don't appreciate what you have, then you will never have enough money.

2. Compare yourself to others. Define your existence based on the cars other people drive and the clothing they wear. Since someone will always have more than you, you will never get rich.

3. Focus on the cost of everything and the value of nothing. Learning that value is irrelevant means you'll never recognize a good opportunity when it's right in front of your face.

Should you focus on making more money or on appreciating what you have?

Money is like oxygen. You need it or you'll die. The right answer is that you should focus on both.

I am not here to hate on wealth or money.

I would challenge you to rethink what it is that you think money can buy, and to ask yourself whether you aren't richer than you think.

Jordan Belfort Straight Line Sales Seminar Review

Jordan Belfort, the *Wolf of Wall Street,* appeared at the Los Angeles Convention Center to give an overview of his Straight Line Sales Seminar. Although the seminar was in many ways a direct rip-off of Tony Robbins' material, Belfort's lectures were interesting, insightful, and far less corny than Robbins'. (Check out: *Jordan Belfort's 4 Secrets to Success.*)

For a lengthy review, including a story about how a groupie made a move on Belfort, go to iTunes or SoundCloud.

If you attend a Jordan Belfort seminar, prepare to take a lot of notes. Belfort jumps all over the place. I took detailed notes of the seminar and have reproduced them below.

The Power of Intention Cannot Be Manifested Without Action.

Belfort spoke of the Law of Attraction as its currently understood in *The Secret* with appropriate dismissiveness. Rather than sit passively by, a person must take action towards his vision. You must move closer to what you want to attract.

Belfort focused on two primary means of self-development. According to Belfort, a person must master his inner and outer world of success.

(The Two Worlds You Must Operate in to Achieve Mastery)

4 Rules of Outer Game

A person must have an understanding of the world around him. You must master these four outer rules of business.

1. Rules of entrepreneurship (fail elegantly, succeed elegantly).

a. Fail elegantly: learn from your mistakes.

b. Succeed elegantly: don't grow too much too fast. To grow, you must learn to sell your vision of the future. Don't delegate immediately. Rather: (1) optimize, (2) systemize, (3) delegate.

2. Marketing (Internet marketing and traditional marketing).

Marketers find buyers, attract traffic, build an email list, etc. Marketers separate prospects from buyers.

3. Sell, influence, and persuade.

Sellers turns buyers into customers. The first person you have to sell is yourself.

4. Multiple streams of income.

Start seeking multiple income sources. You don't need to be rich to start seeking out alternative sources of income.

4 Rules of Inner Game

1. State management (in the moment, how you feel, war paint).

a. Four states winners master: certainty, clarity, courage, confidence.

b. Four states losers master: uncertainty, overwhelmed, fear, self-doubt.

(Physiological / Emotional States)

Note: Matthew McConaughey's "war cry" in Wolf of Wall Street did not come from Jordan Belfort. Rather, that war chant is what Matthew McConaughey himself uses before a scene to get into peak state. When the producers saw McConaughey doing the chant, they asked him to work it into the scene with Leonardo DiCaprio.

(Improving Your Posture Will Increase Your Ability to Change Your State.)

2. Beliefs.

Beliefs are the "bullshit stories you tell yourself."

"People won't follow you if you set a goal. People follow you if you had a vision." – Jordan Belfort

3. Vision-focus.

a. Vision: "Happiness isn't where you are. It's where you think you're heading. You don't have to get rich to feel good. You feel good once you start going for your vision." You have to see it to want it.

b. Focus: learning how to focus on vision rather than on what you're afraid of. Most focus on where they don't want to go, of what they're afraid of. We move in the direction of our focus. We also attract what we focus on.

4. Standards.

Standards are your long term indicator of success, your thermostat, what turns you on and off. Belfort always had high financial standards. He told the story about selling ice cream in the beach. Whereas Belfort's friends were content to sell enough in one week that allowed them to rest all summer, Belfort worked all summer long.

"What people call a work ethic is really just the standard that people hold themselves to." – Jordan Belfort

2 Types of People in the World

1. Reason people.

They always have a reason why they can't do something.

a. A story they tell themselves about why they can't have what they want.

b. Impossibility notion. They are perpetual planners, always planning by never launching.

2. Results people.

They don't tell themselves a story, they take action. If you lack a skill, you go out and get it.

Jordan Belfort used Warren Buffett as an example of an action person. Warren Buffett was terrified of public speaking. He sought out the resources he needed to become a better speaker; namely, a public speaking seminar by Dale Carnegie.

Jordan Belfort on Writing vs. Speaking

Jordan Belfort learned how to write by reading *Bonfire of the Vanities* by Tom Wolfe (Amazon). Belfort modeled his writing off of *Bonfire*. Deconstructed it.

Belfort did the same with *Fear and Loathing in Las Vegas* by Hunter S. Thompson (Amazon).

"You don't have to know your mentors. I didn't know Tom Wolfe." – Jordan Belfort

The Straight Line Sales Method

After going through the rules of inner and outer game, Belfort introduced his Straight Line Selling Method.

A perfect sale (a "lay down," in sales terms) goes in a straight line. You make the call and you close the deal without any objections.

To create a straight line for your product, use backwards planning. Work back from yes. What has to happen in every step leading up to yes?

Call >>>>>>>>>>>>>>>>>>>>>> Close the deal.

Once a client makes an objection, you have veered from the straight line. Objections create a crooked line. The mindset is to answer the objection before returning the buyer back on the straight line.

The first four seconds of conversation made people perceived Jordan in a certain way. His prospects gave him control.

("You have four seconds to establish three things with a customer." – Jordan Belfort)

3 Things to Show a Buyer in the First 4 Seconds of a Sales Call

1. Sharp as a tack.

Show that you are smart and knowledgeable about your subject. When in doubt, "Act as if…"

2. Enthusiastic as hell.

a. Below the surface enthusiasm, be subtle.

b. Show enthusiasm through body language and tone of voice, which are 90 percent of how you make a sale.

3. Expert in your field.

People trust experts. Establish yourself as a trusted authority.

How do you respond to objections that take you off of the straight line?

At Stratton Oakmont, Jordan Belfort was having trouble with his brokers. Although Belfort could sell, he was having trouble teaching his methods to his brokers. Belfort asked them what the problem was. "There are a thousand objections," the Stratton Oakmont brokers would say.

Belfort got up next to his whiteboard. "List them," he told the guys.

The guys were only able to list twelve objections, and many of them were repeats. The objections included: "I don't have money," "It's a bad time to invest," and, "My wife won't let me invest."

Belfort created an answer for each objection and trained his sellers how to overcome these objections.

Mike's Random Observations About Jordan Belfort's Seminar

More cerebral than Tony Robbins. Tony Robbins played too much hokey music. However, Belfort's material comes directly from Tony Robbins. Anyone who has attended a Tony Robbins Seminar will see the similarities.

When I looked around, I noticed that 90 percent of people were not taking notes. Even people who spent time and money to attend Belfort's seminar would not take action and apply what was taught.

There was a get-rich-quick infomercial during the seminar. Someone else held that "lecture." People lined up to sign up for the get-rich-quick scheme.

Overall, the Straight Line Sales Seminar was good information logically presented.

Belfort told a lot of stories. These stories were a bit redundant if you've read *WOWS*. But there are hidden meanings in Belfort's stories. Belfort's mindset is revealed in these stories, even though he doesn't explicitly state his mindset.

Belfort's entrepreneurial mindset was always to look at his bosses and think, "Why am I working for these people rather than doing what they do?"

He spent months with Leonardo DiCaprio and taught DiCaprio his whole straight line sales process. Watch *Wolf of Wall Street* and pay attention to how Leo talks, what he says, etc. Pay especially close attention to DiCaprio's body language in the first close film scene.

Ultimately, the 3+ hour seminar was a sales pitch for his longer seminar and coaching program.

Given what I saw at the seminar, I'd image it's mostly sheep who find themselves at longer seminars with the wolf.

Read more: *The Wolf of Wall Street* (Amazon).

The Wolf of Wall Street Jordan Belfort's "4 Keys for Life Success"

Jordan Belfort, whose life story was adopted in *The Wolf of Wall Street* (read the book here), did not accidentally get rich. His success was the result of his views of himself and the world around him. In a nearly one-hour interview (available at the end of this post), Jordan Belfort shares his four keys for life success. (Jordan Belfort did not follow these 7 Habits of Highly Effective Losers.)

Jordon Belfort's "4 Keys for Life Success" video is interesting to watch not only for Belfort's wisdom, but because it allows you to observe an animated speaker who understands how to use his body effectively when communicating. He also has a somewhat higher-pitched voice, which may surprise some listeners.

Learn How to Control Your State Like the Wolf of Wall Street. Download this podcast.

Unfortunately, the interviewer kept cutting Belfort off to make some banal point. The interviewer also distracted from Belfort's inspirational message by asking for war stories like some groupie. I was more interested in learning Jordan Belfort's four tips for life than I was in hearing the interviewer's points on NLP.

Belfort starts getting going around eleven minutes in, and it gets really good at fifteen minutes in. If you're familiar with Tony Robbins' work, you'll recognize a lot of it in Belfort's talk.

There Are 4 Things You Have to Do to Be Wildly Successful at Anything

Jordan Belfort's Life Tip 1. Vision: The Ability to Create a Clear and Compelling Vision for the Future

According to Belfort, you shouldn't merely set goals. You need something greater than goals. You need a vision.

A goal is something you accomplish. A vision is something you see. It is an entirely new world.

To create a vision, you must "step into [whatever goal it is that you've set] and ask what your world is going to be like." Ask yourself what your world will look like. What will the world look like for yourself, your family, and your friends. If you make a million dollars (a goal), how will your mother's or father's medical care improve (the vision)?

Belfort used Nelson Mandela and Gandhi as examples of visionaries. Mandela and Gandhi didn't merely set goals. They saw entirely new worlds. They then worked towards creating those worlds.

Jordan Belfort's Tip 2. The Ability to Manage Your State: The Way You Feel in the Moment

Your state is how you feel. It's what most of us call our mood.

Being in the right state "allows you to access the resources you have. If you're angry and negative and unresourceful, you can't do anything well." The higher your state, the greater your resources. The lower your state, the scarcer your resources.

Belfort asks you to think about a bad day where you've said to yourself, "I can't believe I said that, I can't believe I did that." On other days you say to yourself, "That was amazing! I got so much done!"

One day you're perfect, one day you suck. That's because of your state. Your state is something you can learn to control. You can put yourself into a resourceful state at will. Being able to control your state is what separates successful people from normal people.

Manage the way you feel in the moment. Find the most resourceful state. For parents the most resourceful state is patience; for traders, its certainty. Fear is a killer.

3 States You Need to Master

1. Certainty: to be certain about that you're doing.

2. Clarity: to be clear and not overwhelmed.

3. Courage: to have a conviction and not let fear stop you.

(Rich people act in the face of fear, whereas poor people run away during fear.)

Jordan Belfort's Tip 3. Manage Your Beliefs and Eliminate Limiting Beliefs

Your beliefs act like a governor on a car. A limiting belief is like putting a governor on the engine of a Ferrari. It slows you down. It stops you from charging forward when you should move forward, and it causes you to move backwards when you should be moving forward.

Parents and teachers spoon-feed us limiting beliefs. Most of them meant well. They gave us limiting beliefs because they were afraid. They didn't want us to believe in ourselves too much. What if we failed?

Belfort would constantly remove the limiting beliefs from his employees' heads by holding two meetings a day. He'd tell his employees, "The moment you walked through this door, the past fell off. You'll start acting like a CEO when you sit behind this desk."

You Are Not Your Past.

Most of our limiting beliefs come from our past experiences. (I mentioned that point during my guest appearance on the Christian McQueen Show.)

Belfort takes a triumphant view on traumatic past life experiences. He observes (at around 41:34 in the interview):

You are not your past, you are the resources and capabilities you glean for it. That is the basis for all change. If you survived the worst of the worse and are still breathing, you can learn from that.

The more crap from your life that you survived, the more likely that you will become great. You must change the way you look at your past. Reverse the angle.

You will find so much power, passion, and internal fortitude from your past if you look at all the horrible things that have happened to you as training for what you must become now. View the past as a prelude to your vision for the future.

Jordan Belfort's Tip 4. Adopt the Right Strategy

You must have the right strategy. (Unfortunately, the interviewer wasted so much time that we didn't get a great elaboration from Belfort.)

Jordan Belfort's Tip 5 (Bonus). Raise Your Standards

To become wildly successful, you must raise your standards. You will not settle for less than what your standards are.

Raise your standards. Decide to never settle for settle for average.

The full video interview where Jordan Belfort shares his 4 key life tips for success is available here:
https://www.youtube.com/watch?feature=player_embedded&v=G3K92uugO9o

How Will You Change Your Business?

The wage slaves are taking the weekend off. Rather than strategize about how to free themselves from the rat race, they are out wasting time. Maybe they have a hangover because they got soooo fucked up last night, man. It was suuuuuuuch a great time.

You are different. You know that your days off are your *on* days. While the bossman is out being nagged by his piggy wife, getting into debt buying stuff he doesn't need, and eating at the Cheesecake Factory, you are planning your Fuck You Exit.

Your day off is your day to focus on freedom, to wake up and say, "I want to change my life."

You can't change your life unless you change your money. Money is like oxygen. Without it, you will die.

What do you need? How will you get it? How will you change your life?

Step 1. What do you need for your business to grow?

Most people suffer from mindset failures. They use sites like *Danger & Play* as self-help porn. Rather than apply the simple lessons, they nod their heads, say "Cool story, bro," and go back to watching cartoons and "prank" videos.

They are looking for distractions because they fear reality. They do not believe in themselves. They have been taught to be good little slaves.

If you are afraid of success, go read the Mindset posts, as what's coming next isn't right for you at this time.

In business, either you do it or someone else does it, but it must get done.

There are many things not getting done at *Danger & Play Holdings*. The work is not getting done due to my own leadership failures. I must take action to make my vision become a reality.

***Gorilla Mindset*:**
- (I have someone working on this.)

Gorilla University:
- Establish an online university with a audio and video series covering topics that men want to learn about. We could have courses on everything from administering TRT, to body language, to meditation, to buying a suit, to keeping cool under pressure, to state control, to anything you want to know.

Gorilla Nootropic:
- Label design.
- Web design.
- Formulation suggestions.
- Social media outreach (i.e., respond intelligently to the invariable Reddit trolls and other "Internet experts" who are going to slander GN.)

YouTube:
- Edit YouTube videos.
- Make my YouTube header look good.
- Add logos onto my videos.
- Create a playlist for my channel.
- Create a trailer for my channel.
- Appear in YouTube videos by demonstrating alpha posture exercises, meditation, and other topics I want to teach.
- Follow me around all day and record stuff we do. We could do some interesting "day in the life" videos.
- Film me juicing veggies and cooking stuff in a Crockpot. We can then upload and edit that onto YouTube.

Danger & Play Podcast:
- Figure out how to upload the podcast as an mp3.

- Create a new logo (gorilla with a microphone or maybe my face).
- Look into alternatives to SoundCloud.
- Create some cool motivational audio files with words and background music.
- Create an entire series on a given subject, sort of like the Great Courses.

Gorilla Mindset Podcast:
- Create a new podcast focusing exclusively on mindset.

Danger & Play:
- A graphics guy or someone who can use Photoshop. I say, "Hey, I want an image of X for an upcoming post," and he delivers.
- Copyediting.
- Moderate the comments.
- Turn posts into mini eBooks.
- Talk to me about post concepts. Keep track of these concepts, create a spreadsheet or checklist, and follow-up to ensure we are getting through them.
- Organize my email box. Ensure that every email (that is not parasitic, asking for something for nothing, or otherwise is stupid and time wasting) gets a response from me.

Fit Juice:
- Take awesome pictures (or use the pictures I take) that we could put into various green juice recipe books.
- Create a bunch of niche juicing site: *Juicing for Athletes, Juicing for Anabolic Steroid Users, Juicing for Jiu Jitsu.*

I have ideas non-stop, but I simply cannot put them into action. Ideas are worthless if you do not put them into practice.

In essence, I need some guys to follow me around 24/7, take notes, record our conversation, and learn to become content creators.

Ideally, the team would start by taking my ideas, creating stuff under my direction, and then learning how the creative process works. They would hone their own respective skills while learning what only I can teach.

After a few weeks or months they would go their merry way, apply the newfound knowledge to their own businesses, and take their lives and businesses to the next level.

Step 2. How will you get what you need for your business to grow?

There are huge business textbooks out there. Ultimately you need three things to make a business work: time, money, and people.

Are you short on money, time, or people? I am short on time and people, but have some money set aside to take D&P to the next level.

I therefore need to free up some time to sit down, strategize, and figure out a way to put my money to good use. (I've been strategizing all morning and will have a call with my consultants at BADNET this weekend.)

What about you? What resource do you need most to change your business?

Step 3. What obstacles do you face?

For some of you, your biggest obstacle is mindset. You're afraid to endure the pain that will always precede growth.

Why are you afraid of success? Why are you afraid of failure? Will you die if your business fails? What is stopping you from doing whatever the fuck you want to do?

Unlike a lot of people, mindset is not my problem. I am delusional. I think D&P can be as big as I want it to be and that only by the resources I put into it limit it.

I am a horrible project manager who has zero interest in hiring a bunch of people from oDesk or Fiverr.

To take D&P to the next level, I need a team that I can check in with every day or so. In person.

Step 4. How will you overcome those obstacles?

I have some ideas for myself, but enough about me.

How will you overcome the biggest obstacles your business faces?

Mindset

Audacity, Audacity, Always Audacity!

What is audacity, and how can you use audacity to get what you want out of life?

The dictionary definition of audacity should draw you in: "Audacity is an insolent form of boldness, especially when imprudent or unconventional. It implies a degree of impudence, but also fearlessness and intrepid daring."

Audacity was the guiding principle of one of the patron saints of *Danger & Play:* General George S. Patton. I live my life by the leadership principles of General George S. Patton (Amazon).

Be audacious in all of your actions.

Audacity came up in the context of a reader question, and I believe it was Freedom and Fulfillment who said "You know you're just a kid from a small town and you were nobody. Your parents were on welfare. You wore filthy dirty clothes, didn't have anything. How is it that you've been to Sheryl Sandberg's house and met Gerry Spence and met all these people?"

And the answer is I read this book in college called *Patton on Leadership* and because of that, General George S. Patton is the closest thing to a patron saint that we would have at *Danger & Play*.

If you're not Catholic, you might not know what a patron saint is, but you'll maybe see people sometimes wear these silver medallions and it'll say "Saint Christopher protect us," right?

Well, the patron saints for me and *Danger & Play* would be Aleksandr Karelin and General Patton. When I look up, I'm like WOW. Yeah, Arnold Schwarzenegger is cool, Tony Robbins is cool, but Patton and Karelin are next level. And these are people who, if there were gods among men, then they would be true gods among men.

And they both were audacious. And I read this book called *Patton on Leadership* and there was a chapter called "Audacity: On Managing the Impossible" and the quote was "Audacity, Audacity, Always Audacity." And Patton would say that. Apparently it came from some other Prussian thinker earlier on.

And you just think, what is audacity? How can you use audacity to your advantage?

Audacity to me means you are standing up and being counted. I'll give you an example of this.

How did I meet Gerry Spence? It was around 2000-2001. I was in law school, in the library watching tapes on how to do a cross-examination. If you are a lawyer, you've probably heard of Irving Younger. This was actually the VHS days. I saw these VHS tapes and thought they were cool; I then I saw that Gerry Spence had a series that cost $400. I asked the law library (again, audacity) if they order them. They said no. Okay then, I'm going to ask Gerry Spence. I'm going to track down Gerry Spence.

Now, this wouldn't work today because you get thousands of emails if you're somebody like Gerry Spence. But I said, "I'm going to ask Gerry Spence if I could get a deal on these tapes or what I can do." I went to his law firm website and of course, they didn't have his email address on there because he was a big celebrity then. I don't know if he's a big celebrity now. Tell me guys, have you heard of Gerry Spence? If not, you should have.

I said, "I'm going to get this guy's email address." So I saw that there were a bunch of contact forms for the associates of the firm, but not for Gerry. So I clicked "View Page Source," and every email address followed a pattern: it was first initial middle initial at [Gerry Spence's law firm] dot com.

It was Gerry L. Spence I believe, so I said "I'm going to send an email to gls at Gerry Spence's law firm dot com and I bet you that's his email address." So I sent him an email. In it, I said, "Gerry Spence, I admire you. You're one of the reasons I went to law school. I've read all your books and I want to get a head start on how to be a trial lawyer and how to cross-examine people and I saw that you have these tapes. My law library won't buy them and the tapes are $400. I can't afford $400. What do you think?"

And he emailed me back. And I was like "Whoa Gerry Spence emailed me back." And he said, "Thank you for your email Michael, I'm forwarding this to my assistant, she will get in touch."

Whoa.

So then his assistant emails me, "Yeah, our hard costs on these are $80, so we'll send you the tapes, and you send us $20/month. Does that work?" And I'm like "Whoa, does that work? Are you kidding me? Yeah! Of course that works. How amazing is this?"

How awesome is that, right? And if you think about it, that was kind of an audacious move on my part, right? Who am I to just email Gerry Spence? I'm nobody. I'm just some random kid in a law school from some small town. And who am I to track him down and basically stalk the guy? That's who I am.

Audacity is like this: "Who do you think you are?"

That's what I want people to say. "Who does Mike think he is?" Right here, that's who I think I am. That's who you're looking at. That's how I think of audacity: I'm going to make these bold and audacious moves. And then I did more than that.

He gave a seminar at the Association of Trial Lawyers of America, the New York meeting of the stars. And he was going to be the keynote speaker. And I said, "I have to meet Gerry Spence." Well, how do I, some kid who doesn't have any money, afford to travel from California to New York to buy a plane ticket or hotel? I said "I'm gonna see Gerry Spence, how am I going to do it?"

The Association of Trial Lawyers of America, like every other sort of public interest organization, want a presence in law schools because they want to get you into their funnel right away. They want you in the ATLA right away. Well, there was no ATLA chapter at my school. So you know what? I said, "I'm going to start an ATLA chapter." So I started an ATLA chapter, sent out an announcement through my law school's newsletter, then met a guy who's remained my lifelong friend to this day. He's made a lot of money with another friend I met in law school that I put him in touch with. And they are just killing it. And I put a note in the newsletter that said, "Hey I want to start ATLA, who wants to start ATLA with me?"

BOOM. He started it with me. Well, now what? I start this private club and because of that I get school funds. And a friend of mine was running for student body association president or student bar association president and I said, "Well, I'm going to help this person get elected."

So I help that person get elected. So I'm now chapter president of a club and I helped a friend get elected, so then I went to SBA and they have all these discretionary funds and I said "Hey you know what, there's this thing going on in New York. You know one of the things is we are at a great law school, but we're still a little bit under the radar and I'm a respectable guy (or at least I was at the time right?). I'm going to fly out to New York to this thing, would you guys maybe buy my plane ticket and maybe give me like $500 for a hotel?"

"Hey, of course!"

So next thing you know, I'm flying out to New York where Gerry Spence is going to be, because why? I'm audacious man. I'm going to do it, right? I'm going to do it. I don't like talking about myself, but I realize that I have to because what I tell you men to do, this is all stuff I've been doing. And this is stuff I still do. So I'm going to go to New York and I'm going to meet Gerry Spence. End of discussion. I found a way. I gotta find a way. Think like no one else thinks. That's audacity. You're going to do it.

Read Patton on Leadership, study General Patton.

He just rampaged through Europe. Destroyed everybody. He would have destroyed Russia. We wouldn't have had a Cold War if it had been for Patton. And of course they killed him, because people don't always like the audacious. Our own government killed him, but that's another story.

So I'm going to go to New York, I'm going to meet Gerry Spence. And what do I do? I go out there, I'm just sort of walking around and I'm in the lunch like "Oh my God." Meeting Gerry Spence was like meeting my hero. I always remember when I met him: chills, goosebumps, my face was flushed red and so I just walked up, I was probably a little sheepish but still I made the audacious move. I know that this guy is important and that I'm a nobody, but I'm just going to go up and introduce myself to him.

So I go up and I say "It's absolutely my honor," and he kind of looked at me like "Well who do you think you are?" Because that's what they look at when you're audacious, "Who do you think you are?"

I said, "You know Gerry, you are absolutely a hero of mine. I'm so proud to meet you and thank you so much for helping me with those VHS tapes. I really appreciate it."

And he's like "Oh, well, thank you." And I said, "Hey can I have my picture taken with you?" And he's like, whoa you're just asking for everything, what more do you want? I was kind of taken aback because he has such a presence that I didn't know he was joking and then he laughed and said "Get over here," and gave me a big hug. If you want to learn charisma, study Gerry Spence.

So I meet him, I get my picture taken with him. So I'm a nobody, I know Gerry Spence. So next thing you know like a year later I went to–Gerry Spence would have the big trial lawyer's college thing, which you had to be a lawyer with like, I don't know, 50 trials to get in. And then he had these little regional seminars, and I said I'm going to go to a regional seminar. Sure enough. I did. So how did I do it? Audacity. I just always found a way.

Another example of audacity, I was working at this asbestos law firm. I'm kind of embarrassed now, but I was young and naïve at the time so don't judge me too harshly. But I was working in an asbestos law firm and I was a law clerk so that would have been before my third year of law school. So I'm like 24 or 25. There was going to be this legislation passed about asbestos reform which we do absolutely need, and if the legislation passed, the law firm would basically shut down. Everybody was afraid. There's fear everywhere. And people didn't know what to do.

So I sent an email to everyone, this is audacious. People were like, "What?" I said, "I interned at a U.S. senator's office in college (which is true). I know from experience that they have certain measurements and that every phone call they get, they view as the equivalent of 200 voters. Every letter they count is like 1,000 voters."

So I sent this email talking about here's how they view things, here's what you can do. Don't just send a big letter signed by 50 people at the same time. Don't let them know that you work for this law firm. Just send a letter from your own letterhead and I sent it. Boom reply all.

And I was working in my little tube rat station or whatever and people were like "Who is this?" Whispers, right? Because people don't like to stand out. Well what happened? So Senator John Edwards, he was a big deal. So next thing you know, I'm at my boss' house because he noticed me, right? Because the big guys are always going to notice and respect audacity. The little people, the flunkies, the peons: they are the ones that want to cut you down. The big guys, they respect the audacity.

Next thing you know, I'm at his house. It was in a place like Napa [California], but it was near Novato. And he lives in an orchard. The guy lives in a freaking wine vineyard. I'm at his house, I'm meeting John Edwards, people are talking about me, blah blah blah, right?

Always, always, always audacious.

A friend of mine, I met because I read his columns, this is back, if you're a law student, in something called LexisNexis. And LexisNexis allows you to search everything. This was before Google. It's better than Google because you can search basically any newspaper that was ever written, any old story. I was searching around for Gerry Spence and I saw this guy had written about Gerry Spence. And I thought, "Well, I want to meet this guy." So I just started sending the guy emails. And when you send a busy person like that emails, this was as email was becoming more popular, you are going to get one or two word responses and you can't take it personally.

I would just say, "Hey I read your column, it's amazing blah blah blah," three paragraphs and he would say "Thanks for writing in." I realize now, because I get a lot of emails, that he wasn't being dismissive. At the time, you are younger and you want to engage right? You respect these people, they are your heroes. And you want to engage but you only have so many hours in the day, right? I'm not even huge and sometimes I just don't have the time to answer all my emails.

I really wish I could.

That's why I do these podcasts and other things, and that way it's like I'm answering the emails eventually, but I'm doing it in a way that everybody can kind of grow together with. I would email him and email him and it was one word sentences. Finally it was like Christmas Break and he said "Hey I'm working on a death penalty appeal in the Supreme Court, I can't pay you, but would you want to help me?"

Sure, come on dude. When you're in law school this is the kind of stuff you salivate for, right? So I was working with him and then next thing you know, I met this big time personal injury lawyer, out in L.A., again because I wrote him a letter. The column my friend wrote said, "Hey, this guy is my best friend and he has this thing where if you tell lawyer jokes, he'll just turn around and leave the room."

And a DEA agent came in and gave a talk at these things called continuing legal education seminars. Because as a lawyer you have to continue your education, you go to these seminars and the guy says, "Oh I'm in a room full of lawyers, oh I mean liars." So this guy, who's a friend of mine got up, turned his back and walked out. So I wrote a letter to the guy and said "I read about this and I just think that's cool. Wow." And I attached my résumé so then I get an email from his assistant saying "Come on in. Talk to us." So I went in, I met him and it was a weird meeting because he asked me a question I wasn't prepared to answer and he goes, "So, what do you want from me?"

I said, "Uh, I don't know." And I didn't necessarily want anything from him, I didn't necessarily want to work for him, I don't know what I wanted at the time. A lot of times you write to these people and you don't know what you want and people who are powerful or rich, they expect you to want something from them. So that's something you need to be prepared to answer. We just talked and I said, "To be honest I don't even know."

He said, "Okay, if you ever want to work for me, you have to read this book called *The Winning Brief* by Bryan Garner." I read *The Winning Brief* and a lot of people say "Oh you're a good writer, blah blah blah."

To the extent that I'm a good writer, it's because I read all of Bryan Garner's works. I've read a lot of books on writing. There are a lot of grammatical errors, I know, in my posts and that's a function of time. I know when I'm making the mistakes, but man, writing takes a long time, and I'm not going to spend two hours editing everything.

So then, that got me growth. What did I want from him? Well, I didn't even know, but he told me to read this book and that book sent me on a whole different journey of my life where now I'm reading, writing, and really trying to be a craftsman. Not a craftsman, an artist. I would say right now that what I do is art. It isn't just stringing a couple sentences together. There's style, there's a voice. When you read this, you know that I wrote it. Well, that just started because this big time lawyer, who I was nobody to, said "Hey man, if you ever want to work for me, you better read this book."

That's because of audacity. I just got up. Stood up. And I reached out to him.

So I had little important encounters with important people all the time and that was because of my audacity.

Even now, I'm audacious, and I'll give you another example. I'm in this, I guess you could call it a networking group and I'm basically bottom of the barrel there. Have you ever heard of Hands Across America? You younger guys haven't. Go Google Hands Across America. It's absolutely amazing. He's a member. The guy who gave Steve Jobs his first job is there. This guy, he invented the video game. I'm nobody, right? Which I like. A lot of the problems I'm having, I'm having more and more trouble finding things to read where it's like, that feeds my soul.

I view what I do as I'm feeding your souls and you're feeding my soul and everybody is feeding each other's souls, you know? The higher you get and the higher your soul gets, the higher in the mountain you have to climb.

So I'm like, I just need to be at the bottom of another mountain, where I'm just a nobody, you know? So I just joined this group and man, I'm nobody in this group. But I'm still audacious. There's a point in the group where they say, "Does anybody have any announcements?"

And guys are always pitching their businesses. So I raised my hand. "What's your announcement? Stand up."

"I run this website, one-man operation, I do everything, last month I had X page views. Best month ever." So a lot of people were like, wow. I haven't released my traffic yet, but when I do, a lot of people are going to be surprised. And I said, okay, cool. So next thing you know, at the end of it, a guy comes up to me, an older guy that would have never have talked to me and he's the founder of *L.A. Weekly*. If I had emailed that guy asking for a meeting, he never would have talked to me. This is a very important person. And he's like, "How do you get so many page views? Here I have this other site I'm trying to build up; it's a site about drug addiction."

So the next thing you know, he's showing me the mobile version of his site, I'm showing him the mobile version of my site.

We're talking about thumbnails and headlines, and then he said, "Well, you know the new thing is, you gotta put the thumbnail on the image. That actually gets more views and more clicks than the headline next to the images."

"I say, yeah I know, but I can't do it with my current theme." And then we start talking about A/B testing things, and it's just crazy, right? This guy never would have noticed me. A couple weeks later I was at a meeting and the guy who founded the Quest Bars stood up and gave a little talk. I wrote about that at *Danger & Play* and a couple of people are like, "Where do I get them?" And a couple of people are jibber-jabbering and I say, yeah I've had one or two a week and everybody was trying to talk over me so I just stood up.

Because that's what you do right?
Audacity.

If everybody's talking over each other and sitting down, stand up. Stand up like a man. "Who does this guy think he is?" This is who he is. I'm going to stand up. So I stood up and I just said, "Hey man, I love your bars. They are amazing, I eat one or two a day." And then I turned to address the whole audience when you talk, you know? Based on the theater seating, you don't just want to do a laser beam at the one guy, you want to turn and make sure you are talking to everybody to include them.

I said "I eat one or two a day. Quest Bars are amazing. They don't spike your blood sugar. What this man has is amazing. Thank you so much. You're a visionary."

And then I sat down.

Now what did that get me? Is the guy going to say something, blah blah blah? No, it isn't about what it gets me. It got me noticed, right? Now, people notice me. Sure, when you are audacious, people are going to look at you a little weird. Or maybe not like you.

But here's what you men have to understand:
You don't need everybody to like you.

I don't need a single woman to read *Danger & Play*. I don't need 95% of men to read *Danger & Play*. If one percent of the men in the world with Internet access read *Danger & Play*, it would be too much of a monster site for me to handle, I wouldn't even know how to handle the traffic. So I'm audacious even at *Danger & Play*. People say, "I can't believe you said that or I can't believe you wrote that."

That's how you want people to think of you: "I can't believe he said that. It's bracing. Who is this guy?" It's General Patton, man. It's Aleksandr Karelin. It's, you're audacious, you're bold. You stand up and be counted. People notice you and again, you don't need everybody to like you. 99 percent of the people can hate me. One percent can love. That's all I need: the one percent. I mean, look at you guys listening in, you know?

We're growing together like crazy. The comments are amazing. People want a forum so they can talk to each other. A bunch of people have met and made great connections at the meet-ups we've been having. This is it, baby. We haven't even taken things full-blast. I'm just a one-man guy on a shoestring operation. I do all my own web design. I do all my back-end stuff, I edit all my podcasts. Right now I'm doing a podcast; I'm not in a studio. I'm in my living room. I'm on a Snowball. I'm not paying anybody for anything other than the podcast transcriptions.

And look at how much we're growing right? Because we have audacity.
Audacity means I do this damn podcast, right?

"Who is this guy to do a podcast?"
"Who is this guy to take on these big names?"

"Who is this guy to call anyone out?"

It's audacity.

So there you go.

How do you meet people? How do you live your life? How do you get what you want out of life?

Read about General Patton. Go get that book, *Patton on Leadership.*

Go on YouTube and type in, "Patton speech," and you see George C. Scott standing in front of the big American flag.

If you just listen to that, you can't not be inspired.

Go look at Aleksandr Karelin, I think it's called the Karelin lift, just pick up 300-pound guys and just flip them over his shoulder and slam them into the ground. It was actually his special lift.

And speaking of audacity, the Olympic committee had to change the rules and rig it so that he wouldn't win the gold medal in his final game. He didn't lose a match or have a point scored against him for eleven years. Because of his audacity.

So they changed the rules. So there's a dark side to audacity. People might try to kill you. George Patton? Murdered. Aleksandr Karelin? The rules were changed, rigged so that he couldn't win that final gold medal. Me? There are people coming after me, but you know what?

Come at me.

I don't care.

I love it.

This is when I l feel alive.

I feel alive when the barbarians are just coming at me and attacking.

If you think about *300* and the Spartans. Even though there were a thousand or whatever. Read *Gates of Fire.* THAT'S, that's audacity. There's a whole army coming at you, and you just stand one by one next to your brother and you just say "Come at me."

That's audacity right there.

So that's how I want you to start thinking about life.

I know I use the term aggression and dominance and everything else, but when it comes right down to it, I only live by one word.

That one word is audacity.

So before we go, let's look at the actual definition of it because I think it's such a cool definition.

This is on Wikiquote:

"Audacity is an insolent form of boldness, especially when imprudent or unconventional. It implies a degree of impudence, but also fearlessness and intrepid daring."

How awesome is that?

Isn't that what you want to be?

Be audacious.

Become Obsessed to the Point of Madness

Do you want to know the secret to giving up all of your vices? Do you know why you have a bunch of bad habits in the first place?

I will tell you why, and my answer isn't the one self-help gurus will give.

There is a sad secret that you won't admit to yourself.

You have vices because you are aimless. Your life has no purpose.

You are simply existing. You are riding whatever wave life throws at you instead of making your own waves.

I have a solution. It is a solution that every loser and hater will tell you is wrong.

Become obsessed.

Obsession is Not a Bad Word.

Losers will tell you that obsession is a bad thing. You should have balance. That is why they are losers. Consider the average man.

("Will wife/daddy/the boss man let me play with my train set later?")

Here is what occupies the thoughts of the average man:

- What is my girlfriend/wife doing right now? Is she cheating on me? Why hasn't she texted me all day?!
- What's up with the higher-ups? That email my boss sent me was vague. Does he like me?
- Aimlessly surf the web.
- What's for lunch?

- Feel tired after eating big lunch.
- Is it 5 o'clock yet?
- Look for nearby microbrew to can display superior knowledge of hops, malt, and barley to other aimless dorks.
- TV time!

The average man is just trying to fill up his day with distractions. He is, as the saying goes, *"just killing time."*

(There is no danger. There is no play. There is only tedium and quiet desperation.)

Become Obsessed with Excellence.

Let me tell you what happened when I became obsessed with taking *Danger & Play* to the next level.

- I don't *want* to get drunk.
- I don't *want* to watch porn.
- I don't *want* to bang random bar skanks. When the girls at the coffee shop couch nuzzle closer to my disgusting muscles, I give them an annoyed look.

Because I am on a mission, it hasn't taken me any willpower at all to rid myself of these filthy habits. I don't have any magic tricks for you. I simply don't have time for nonsense because I am thinking about too many other things.

I do everything for D&P and outsource nothing.

I write/edit every word, edit every podcast, design the page, and handle the back-end crap. Running a website involves a lot of back-end stuff that isn't always fun:

- What is a bounce rate, how does it impact my SEO and what are the best WordPress apps to decrease it? Is Alexa legit; they don't even know what search terms people are using to find me. Disqus? Jetpack? What is an SSL and private IP address and do I need them?
- Write newsletter.

- Post to social media.
- Record and upload podcasts.
- I'm committed to helping every man who comes to D&P but can barely keep up with reader emails.
- Do I sit on this post for a few days until traffic drops or keep juicing my stats?
- What happened to the day!? Time to hit the gym!

Now instead of breaking myself of bad habits that impeded my success, I am becoming a victim of my own success.

I have too many posts and too many podcasts in the works and I'm overwhelming my readers with original content. Let's do a separate post linking to and annotating some posts.

When you become obsessed, you develop tunnel vision. Nothing else matters. You simply don't have to "break yourself free of bad habits" because those bad habits cannot compare to your obsession. Find your obsession and everything else will fall into line.

What is your obsession? Do you have one? If not, what are you going to do to change that – starting today?

Think Like No One Else Thinks

What does inattentional blindness—a concept from cognitive psychology—have to do with the unconscious mind, racism, game, and politics? Continue reading below.

Think Like No One Else Thinks by Noticing What No One Else Notices

So here's what happened and here's where I'm going to go. I was at the St. Louis Airport on a long layover because my flight was delayed. And I said, well, I'm going to sit down and do a podcast. The podcast was going to be on using art to unlock your unconscious mind and to realize your unconscious desires. It's actually going to be a really cool podcast. We're going to talk about the work of Carl Jung and a book called *King, Warrior, Magician, Lover* and we're going to tie that into how you can find your unconscious mind.

The reason we're going to do this podcast first is, I noticed something that I had never noticed before. Which was, the freaking speakers, they are always on. There is always some dumb announcement going on and it's actually much louder and more annoying than I ever thought. And I had always tuned that out. And think about it…

How many things do we tune out that are always there, and what does that do to our unconscious minds and how does that impact our unconscious thoughts?

The cognitive science behind this, it's a well-studied concept and it's called **inattentional blindness**. And if you pull up the Wikipedia, "Inattentional blindness, also known as perceptual blindness, is categorized as a psychological lack of attention and is not associated with any vision defects or deficits."

What does that mean? You walk around and you notice one thing, but you don't notice a bunch of other things even though these other things might be extremely easy to see. For example, there was an experiment where the researchers had the subject sit and watch a bunch of people dribbling on a basketball court and they said to count the number of dribbles on the basketball court. Dribble dribble dribble dribble and everybody said, "Oh I got eleven, is that right?" You know, because we want to be right. And they said "Yeah, great, that was the right number." But that wasn't the experiment. The experiment was, there was a woman who came out, and she was in like a Victorian-style dress with an umbrella and she walked right across the basketball court and almost nobody noticed that.

There was a funny spoof of that in a beer commercial, and I'll try to link to that at *Danger & Play* when I do my show notes, assuming I can find it. The same thing happened, they had people dribbling a basketball and a guy comes out in a gorilla suit, and you don't see the gorilla suit and there's the punchline. You didn't see the gorilla.

Now where is this all headed? I thought about something five minutes ago that can really help us and here's how it can help us.

If you want to be like other people and you want to see the world differently from other people, then you have to pay attention to things other people don't pay attention to.

I just thought of a really cool exercise. On any given day, spot something new or novel. So I said, I'm just going to pay attention to everything that is white. Why white? No reason, that's just the first thing that came to my head, like a lot of these podcasts. Some random thought just comes into my head and I just try to develop it.

You know, I'm in my living room right now and there's white shoelaces, there's white on the bottom of the shoes. I got these boat shoes over there, there are the white laces. Oh, there's a white box over there. These gummy fibers are white. There's a white label on the protein powder. So suddenly, now I'm only noticing everything that's white.

Now you might think "Think is a pointless exercise. What is it getting at?" But we are getting at two bigger concepts.

Thinking differently means you notice things other people don't notice.

If you are like me and everyone else in this world, you are only noticing a few things. And often the only things you are noticing are what people are trying to get you to notice. Think about the original experiment, "Hey count the dribbles," right? So you are paying attention to what somebody else told you to. When the joke was on you, right? There was a woman in a dress and they snuck her right by you. It's almost like magic, isn't it?

Think about politics. Pay attention: right, left, right, left. Are you liberal? Democrat? Liberal? Democrat? That's what they want you to pay attention to. But then watch how people are living in our country, right? Look at the concentration of media ownership and how only a few mega conglomerates own all the papers and they can control the news.

Look at what isn't covered in the news. Go to a website called *ProjectCensored.org* that covers the 25 most censored stories and some of them are a little bit oddball but, some of them are things that you think "WOW why isn't anybody talking about this?" Well it's because of the power elite and the people who are really running this country have tuned in to our inattentional blindness. They have us arguing with one another about what is essentially nonsense.

An example of this, how we can get past this is, I had a meet-up in New York and a meet up in DC and I met with a bunch of *Danger & Play* readers. It was the first time I had done anything like that, it was a really good time and really good success. I think I'm going to do more.

Well, I don't know what anybody's politics are, because I didn't ask. One guy at the New York meet-up said "Man it's nice, I look around and there's actually like some other black guys here you know? Or some other brown people. It's not just mostly white guys." And I said "Well yeah, that's because I don't allow any racism at *Danger & Play* at all. Period. Racism comment deleted."

And for the longest time it was because people thought I was black. So I went with the joke. "Yeah, I'm a black guy, I got the swagger of a black guy and I'm going to be banging all your white girlfriends." And the reason I believe that is because, if you are listening to *Danger & Play*, and reading *Danger & Play*, we are the oppressed. We are the ones who have the world against us. We are in a world where they want us to be less masculine. They want us to have low testosterone, they want us to have cognitive deficits. They want us to just be sick, weak, and feeble. So why in the hell would anybody at *Danger & Play* have a problem with a black guy, or a brown guy, or a Democrat or a Republican, or a liberal or a conservative?

Why would that even matter? That's not the game, right? We're playing their game by doing this. We're paying attention to shit that they want us to pay attention to while they are ruining our society, right? While they are ruining our lives. So think about that.

Think about how you can notice things that other people aren't noticing on a higher, more abstract level, such as how the political game really is.

By starting to notice things other people aren't noticing. How many times do you see white in the room? How many BMWs do you see on the road? How many Jeep Cherokees do you see on the road? Pick anything, it really doesn't matter. This will also make you more successful.

Well I'm not going to do one of those things like, "Gee Mike, well, how do you notice things other people don't notice?" and act like I'm some kind of a cool guy, but if you want to think differently, all I do is I've noticed things other people don't notice. There is no magic to what I do. I'm no kind of super genius. You know, my mom sent me, I don't why she did it… I guess that's just what moms do. A few years ago she sent me back one of my report cards and standardized test when I was like a little kid and all my IQ tests or whatever had put me in 83rd percentile, 88th percentile. You know, a decent smart enough kid, but I don't think anybody would think that I was just kind of that smart. People probably think I'm a little bit smarter than that, but on those so-called standardized tests, yeah you know, smart kid. Above average, nothing special.

I notice things that other people don't notice and that's because I pay attention to things others don't pay attention to.

Think about how this relates to our last podcast, where we talked about the power of active engagement. You are looking at one thing, and you are noticing things that other people don't notice, and that's because you are actively engaged in everything. Remember I said that I just stare at my website and I just look and look and I look and I look. I'm paying attention to everything and I'm paying attention to nothing at the same time. And because of that, I notice things that other people maybe wouldn't notice. And I see things that other people wouldn't see.

There's no magic. You just flip your phone down, don't listen to any outside influences, and you just pay attention to something.

It's actually a good writing exercise too. If you read books on writing, one guy said to pick up an ink pen and just look at it.

Think, "How would I describe the ink pen?" You would talk about the roundness of it. The texture on the handle. The length of it. The color. How it feels in a person's hands. You just do that for an ink pen and go write 500 words on an ink pen. If you can write 500 words on an ink pen and describe it in a vivid, engaging manner... what about when you have something interesting to write about, right?

What if you have something like character development? I don't do fiction, but that's a great way; if you start writing about fictional characters, you start to notice everything about a person. You notice the body language, the posture, you can use that in meeting women. Does a girl crinkle her eyes a certain way when she talks? Well I bet you nobody else has told her that. Maybe she crinkles her eyes when she smiles. What do you think if you were just another guy trying to get a phone number? Maybe you notice something about this girl that nobody else has ever noticed. Do you think you might connect on a little bit of a deeper level? Maybe it's something she noticed about herself and she wishes other people had noticed.

Now what?

You are looking at things in a way that other people aren't, so you are differentiating yourself from every other schlub.

It applies to every area of your life. It applies to entrepreneurialism. That's all the most successful businesses are; they notice things that other people didn't notice. And because of that, they were able to come up with solutions that other people weren't able to come up with.

So what you want to do is train your mind to start noticing what other people don't.

Start off very basic. Again, maybe colors. Maybe textures. Maybe the types of cars that people drive and then start to get a little bit deeper and see how that affects you. And then think even more deeply about the subject and think about how our unconscious mind is taking in everything. Even if our conscious mind isn't aware of it, our unconscious mind is aware of it.

And we're going to talk about how that relates to frame control and the origins of thoughts.

Think about this: where do your thoughts come from? They don't just appear from nowhere. They come from your environment, from your civilization, from your culture. If you live in a certain type of culture, you are going to have certain religious beliefs. And you are going to fight with people tooth and nail and that your religion is right and everyone else if going to die and go to hell… well, where do those thoughts come from? They came from your culture. You didn't come up with them.

Where did your morality come from? There is probably some general universal morality that we can all kind of agree on, but where did monogamy as a moral rather than a situational value come from? Why is monogamy moral and polygamy immoral? Well, it's because of our culture. That came from outside of you, that gets imprinted into your unconscious mind.

Why do you feel crappy about yourself? A lot of times, it's because thoughts got into your unconscious mind from your parents, your teachers, from the government, from the establishment, from the Man. Or today, there's no "the Man," there's "the Woman." And it's completely ruined and wrecked your mind and you weren't even attentive of that.

So where is this all going? Well, if you want to be a better thinker, if you want to control what your unconscious encounters… the best way to control what your unconscious encounters, control your environment.

Regular readers who read *Danger & Play* know I'm real big on not having friends who are losers. You can't have friends who are "do nothings." Even if they are "nice guys," you can't have them in your life and that's because their unconscious attitudes, behaviors, and desires are going to get into your unconscious

155

mind. And it will get into your unconscious mind, again, in a way that you won't even notice because of inattentional blindness.

Tony Robbins Unleash the Power Within Seminar Review

Day 1

Why do some people take action whereas most do not? Why would most men rather watch Internet porn than go to the bar and meet girls? Why do men hate on you when they find out you are bettering yourself by lifting weights, reading books, and generally kicking ass?

In a word, it's all due to fear.

Tony introduces how fear is the life killer.

Tony Robbins believes that fear is the primary driver of human behavior. We live our lives based on fear. Fear controls us. It stops us. FEAR means, "Fuck everything and run away!"

Thus day 1 of Unleash the Power Within is about learning more about fear and how to conquer it.

Fear results from one of three sources: (1) a pattern of physiology, (2) a pattern of focus, or (3) a pattern of language. That makes a lot of sense when you consider why most people never take action.

People are fearful because their body language is poor. They shoulders slump and they generally walk around like beta males who are afraid of making eye contact with women. By changing your body language alone, you can reduce your fear. (However, to fully master your fear, you need to control all three sources that cause the state of fear.)

People also become fearful based on the strength of language. Most of us tend to exaggerate our problems. Someone who is having a bad day will not say, "Meh, today is sorta off," but instead will say, "I'm so depressed." By using the loaded term, depressed, the person becomes more fearful of whatever it is that is causing the underlying emotion.

A man who gets rejected by 9 women will say, "I am a FAILURE with women!" rather than recognizing the truth, "Even the best looking men occasionally get skunked. I'm just burning through the women who aren't my type in order to find the ones who are. No big deal."

All human beings fear rejection, so rejection isn't a word a player should even have in his mental vocabulary. Otherwise you will think, "Damn, I got rejected again," which will cause you to become more fearful. The better response is to say, "I guess she had a boyfriend." I have long said that no woman ever rejects men. The only women who aren't interested in me are lesbians or in happy relationships. By taking on that mindset many moons ago, the sting of rejection went away long ago.

Should you attend a Tony Robbins Seminar?

I've long been a fan of Robbins' content, first studying it in 2000. If you've read much into NLP and the general "science of success," a lot of the stuff will be very basic.

Even though I had a lot of background knowledge about NLP and a success mindset, I learned some very useful and "immediately actionable" knowledge.

Your blueprint.

Robbins big thing is to teach that your life has to match your blueprint. My blueprint has always been accurate. If you're a man who maximizes what it means to be a man, you'll generally succeed. Go to the gym, make some money, don't be a pussy, read a book now and then, do something dangerous, get a little play, don't' whine, and generally the rest will fall into place. My rules are consistent with my life. My blueprint is fine so I don't experience unhappiness that so many seem to have.

State control.

Robbins also focuses a lot on what he calls "state," which is what the rest of us would call "mood." Without realizing it, I would passively accept my state like a dirt bag beta male. If I didn't want to do something (i.e., I wasn't in the "mood" or "state" to perform a task), I'd say, "That's not really my thing," or, "I'm an adult. I don't have to do things I don't want to do."

While it's true that no one can force me to do anything, it's equally true that my mind was doing a lot of rationalization. Sometimes I would let me state control whether or not I'd have fun, whether or not I'd see friends, or whether or not I'd do something fun.

I was too passively accepting my state rather than recognizing that my state is something that I can change. There's no wrong state per se. If I want to feel angry, great. If I want to stay home on a Friday night, that's my right as a free man.

But I have to be honest with myself. Am I being a passive beta male about my own emotions? Should I change my state to that of an outgoing person with a lot of energy before turning down invitations to hang? If I change my state and still want to stay in, then my emotions are not controlling me. But if a state change compels me to leave the house, then I was being an insufferable weakling.

State is affected by language/meaning you assign to words, focus, and physiology.

I rarely paid attention to state outside of the gym. I'd always, without calling it a "state change," change my feelings in the gym. If my legs hurt or I felt like a workout was hard, my state would change, "If you die, you die. Who cares? If you can't do another rep and the weight falls, who cares. Keep pushing."

I would often go into the gym after long work weeks of getting my ass kicked. The first 15-20 minutes of the workout would suck. It would be a time of self-doubt and beta questions. "Why are you even here? You're not trying to be a pro bodybuilder. This is stupid. Go him and rest. You can always come back tomorrow."

By staying at the gym and controlling my physiology by lifting even when it was boring and hurt, my state would change. I HAVE NEVER LEFT THE GYM FEELING WORSE THAN WHEN I ARRIVED AT THE GYM. I would always tell myself that on bad days. "Have you ever felt worse after a workout? No. So keep working out until you get into a right state of mind."

Sometimes this would mean doing 5-10 sets of the same exercise. I'd be too demoralized to train, so I'd get on the Hammer Strength back blast, load on some plates, take unusually lost rest intervals, and just keep doing sets of 10-15 until my vagina got the sand out of it. It always worked and then the workout would be great.

Yet outside of the gym, I wouldn't pay much attention to state. If a friend texted me to hang out, even if this was a good friend, if I wasn't in the mood then I'd just ignore the text or say not. Yet maybe I should have tried to change my state. Maybe I would have wanted to hang out?

My default state is anger

Even though my anger instills fear, it's actually I who am being weak. If my default state is anger and my anger controls me, then I am ruled by emotions. Should I perhaps try getting into the state of a relaxed or happy person? Simply accepting my state without questioning it makes me the same as a woman who is ruled by her feelings.

You can change state using physiology (keep lifting until your mind gets right) and also by a change in focus.

Your focus determines what you feel. If you focus on Internet porn, you will feel lust. If you focus on someone's nicer car, house, or lifestyle, then you will feel jealousy.

If you focus on your problems and navel gaze all day about every injustice, you will feel anger, anxiety, and depression.

To change how you feel is to change your focus. Everyone has had this experience: You're angry about some real or perceived slight someone gave you. Then you see a guy in a wheel chair. Immediately you think, "Damn, I am lucky to be able to walk. I should go to the gym and stop being a whiny cunt."

That's a state change brought on by a change in your focus. You focused on someone else's real problems instead of your bullshit problems. That changed how you felt. You still were having the exact same "shitty day" or whatever, and yet you didn't feel so crappy. That's because the focus shifted from your own petty life to something else.

Thus, "Change your focus, change how you feel."

Thoughts after the end of the first day.

Robbins is the real deal. He was building a resort on Fiji for his private clients…when he was 26. The guy is an apex alpha on Arnold Schwarzenegger's level. If you are so smug and self-satisfied that your mind closes to Tony Robbins, you are a delusional little hater who will do little in life.

If you go into Unleash the Power Within with the right mindset, you will find great value. Since I went with a friend, we got a BOGO discount. Join the email list and you'll get notified about the buy-one-get-one free discount. I think Executive level seats (which are more than adequate, as every seat is good) were around $650 and General Admission were around $550.

Since it's a self-contained seminar, that's and extremely good value. Plus, maybe you'll connect with some legit people who want more out of life.

Day 2

Day 1 of Unleash the Power Within did not end until 2 a.m. Since Day 1 was about conquering fears, the night ended with the infamous fire walk.

The fire walk wasn't a fear I needed to overcome. It's basically impossible to get burned during the fire walk unless you make a mistake. You know what's terrifying? 20 Rep Squats – because you know that's going to hurt, badly, and that you might pass out, might puke, and that your legs will be sore for days afterward. I stayed for the walk because it was part of the experience.

I'm a believer in, "Trust the process." If you're going to a seminar, trust the process. If you don't like it later, no big deal. You don't have to leave with the process. But listen to what you are told and do what you are told for a few hours or days.

The walk was meh for me, but people were super excited.

Day 2 began with the day's speaker, a Tony Robbins' protégé, opening with, "Good morning fire walkers!" The crowd erupted with cheers. People were feeling it. Good for them.

Since Robbins can't talk for 4 days straight, he has a stand-in. During Day 2, his long-time associate leads the group through the exercises in the workbooks. Tony Robbins also appears via a pre-recorded lecture.

Day 1 was about discovering your fears, conquering your fears, and changing your state. Day 2 was about connecting with others.

During Day 2 we performed numerous mirroring exercises and learned about rapport. This stuff was very basic to me. However, the exercises were a powerful reminder of this: If you go into an interaction with the mindset (or state, see Day 1's write-up) that you will connect with this person, your entire demeanor changes. Your tone of voice is stronger. Your words are more pronounced. Your body language is stronger and your moves are more confident.

Rapport skills are like any other skill. If you don't use them, you will lose them. Most guys in the game spend a lot of time trying to show disinterest to women. This can unfortunately harm a guy's professional life since he takes that state into his office. What works for the game on American women is different from what works in the office – where eagerness is often rewarded.

Be mindful of those states. If you're in a bad state, change it.

Day 2's materials also included coverage of business development skills. The lectures were extremely useful. There was a blueprint for people building a business to follow that included a lot of things I had forgotten or overlooked.

During the business skills session, they also had us stop to think, "What is your x-factor?" That is, what makes you different from every other doctor, lawyer, accountant, insurance salesman, personal trainer, or investment banker?

Tony Robbins remains bearish on the overall economy and believes that only the exceptional will achieve good results. To become exceptional, you must discover your x-factor.

Day 2 was cool, although Day 3 was my favorite.

Day 3

In behavioral economics you often encounter the concept of loss aversion. For reasons probably having to deal with evolution (losing territory means losing status, which in the wild means you're dead meat), we experience far great pain when losing something than we feel joy when gaining something.

Consider that most of us have been in horrible relationships, had crappy jobs, and maybe even had a shitty self-outlook. Why not change? Changing means you're losing something to gain something else. Logically you should want to change your pathetic self to become a more heroic self, but the fear of losing whatever little you have leads to inaction.

In order to get a person to change, it's usually not enough to show a person what he will gain. People only generally change when they have hit rock bottom and fear losing more of their life's savings, their friends or their sense of self.

Tony Robbins has found a way to work around the problem of loss aversion.

Not Changing Will Cost You

Although we don't often think of it this way, our current body is borrowed from our future body. Someday the person you are today is going to get examined by the person who is 10, 20, or 30 years older. Your old man self will want to know you didn't save for retirement, why you didn't take care better of your knees, and why you didn't experience more out of life when you had the energy. (Although memories are not substation for the present, one day all any of us will have are memories.)

What negative behaviors do you have today? What are those going to cost you in 5, 10, and 20 years?

Consider someone who is fat and eats a diet of processed foods. His lifestyle is going to cost him opportunities for sex. It's going to cost him bodily decay. It's going to make him miss out on the ability to feel good when he is older. The fat person will have missed out on so much because of his negative behaviors. Not changing is costly.

Or maybe you're mean to your wife (or ex-wife). That's going to cost you intimacy. It's also going to sour any relationship you might have had with your children. Children who grow into adults don't love a man who mentally or physically abuses their mother.

Or maybe you won't take any business risks. People are terrified of risk. ("What if I fail," is loss aversion causing you to doubt yourself.) Yet what's the alternative – working for the man like a corporate slave your whole life, having to call in sick to some superior when you're not going to be at the office, wondering if you're breaking some HR rule, censoring yourself for fear of losing your job?

Through visualization techniques (you need to attend the seminar to experience the concepts fully), you're forced to be confronted with everything your negative behaviors will have cost you. Since we usually don't respond to rewards but instead seek to avoid punishment, these techniques are a breakthrough for most.

Limiting Beliefs

"A belief is something about the world that you believe to be true." Limiting beliefs are a way to protect ourselves from taking any risk. We accept limiting beliefs in order to avoid our own weaknesses and insecurities. They allow us to pretend we are not cowards.

How many men, when receiving obvious buying signals from a woman, will say, "Oh, she's not looking at me?" Men tell themselves that rather than take a risk of getting reject. (That's loss aversion, yet again.)

A short man will conclude that men under 6 foot are unable to date attractive women. By accepting this belief he is freed from doing the hard work of approaching and meeting women.

Nearly all limiting beliefs take on a certain form: "I'm not supposed to be x." Rather than undertake the extremely hard work most of us require in order to achieve x, we use our limiting belief as a cop out. "I'm just not designed that way." That gives us an excuse to give up, which is easy.

If men who claim they can't be x spent as much time working through cognitive behavioral therapy work book as they do brooding over their problems, they would find x. But that's hard as fuck. No thanks. I'm gonna sit here and feel sorry for myself!

My own personal limiting belief is that I'm just a low energy, naturally introverted guy.

After outlining your limiting beliefs, you next need to ask what those beliefs are costing you.

Since I was 14 people told me I could start a cult. I have natural charisma. I would be much richer if instead of avoiding human interaction I embraced it. My limiting belief has cost me a lot of money and opportunities.

Most of the time our limiting beliefs are false. Am I naturally low energy or just childish? A little kid says, "I don't want to do that," based on nothing more than his transient feeling or mood. Isn't it pathetic and unmanly to be a petulant child who won't do anything he doesn't want to do? Most of the time we just reel against the unfamiliar. It's not that we wouldn't enjoy the experience. It's that we're being bratty punks who should be smacked in the mouth.

I am not "naturally" low energy. I'm just a childish whiner who gets into moods and then lets my moods control me. That is absolutely revolting and henceforth unacceptable.

Even when a limiting belief is not false, there's no need for it to rule you. So what if guys who are taller meet more women. That doesn't mean no attractive women will like a guy like you. You will have to work harder than others, but if you work hard enough, you will realize that your limiting belief is actually false.

Wrapping Up

Robbins is known as a "motivational speaker" and "positive thinker." Bullshit. He forces you to look at the negative garbage that's deep within your unconscious. Most people lack the courage to attend a seminar and work through their issues.

He is a positive thinker in the sense that he believes all of us have far more potential than we realize. He believes if we change our behavior and destroy our limiting beliefs, it will be possible for us to achieve great things.

Is he right? I certainly think so. Long before knowing anything about Robbins, I was able to overcome some traumatic experiences by welcoming pain.

What if instead of fearing pain like a little bitch and crying about every stupid problem you have, you told yourself, "Growth requires pain." That is the moral of Conan the Barbarian and is the answer to the Riddle of Steel.

Your behaviors would immediately change, wouldn't they? Instead of being a weak loser who continued repeating the same patterns of behavior that have led to the rut you're in, you'd change your behaviors.

After changing your behaviors, you'd notice something "magical" happening. Suddenly your very mood would change.

While a lot of guys think they are "too cool" for Tony Robbins, the truth is that most guys aren't man enough to examine the weaknesses within themselves and to take immediate and radical action to change their lives.

In America everyone wants to be a birthday boy at his very own pity party.

My view has always been different. You are the lowest life form of a man if you live in a condition worthy of pity.. Dogs left by their owners in animal shelters are pitiable. Children who are abused are pitiable. They lack the ability to change their environments and my heart truly feels for them.

Are you a stray dog who is at the shelter after your owner's house was foreclosed? Do you feel anxious and abandoned while you sleep on a stone concrete floor rather than on a comfortable dog bed or in a bed with your owner? Are you nothing more than a child who hides after his alcoholic father has had too much to drink? Is that really who you are?

How can you look yourself in the mirror as a man when others have pity for you? How can you actively seek out pity and then call yourself a man?

Robbins offers many useful strategies and in the future I likely won't allow anyone to complain about anything unless they've gone to one of his seminars.

The irony is that most men think they are "too fucking cool" to attend a Tony Robbins seminar. Yet moping around the house is cool? Crying and screaming and having childish outbursts about stupid shit is cool?

Maybe my definition of cool differs from some, but I fail to see how wallowing in self-misery is somehow more cool than taking action to change your life.

Call me uncool if you like, but I'm a believer. Unleash the Power Within was my first Tony Robbins seminar and it won't be my last. I was able to begin understanding how negative behavior patterns have cost me success and pleasures.

The work has just begun. I welcome the new challenge.

Whether you decide to continue feeling sorry for yourself or changing your life is, of course, up to you.

How to Set and Achieve Goals (and the Limits of Will Power)

Gorilla Shrewdness #2

This may come as a surprise to you, but I probably have less willpower than most. It's true. I tend to be lazy and overeat. I also enjoy sleeping.

Even without any willpower, I have somehow been able to make some interesting things happen in my life. What's my secret?

I've been able to develop more willpower by working *with* rather than *against* my unconscious mind. I was talking to Dr. Jeremy about how I play tricks on my lizard brain, and he showed me that there's a lot of science behind these tricks. We thought it would be a good idea to have another Gorilla Shrewdness roundtable. (Check out our first one: Testosterone: The Mind-Body Connection.)

<u>Mike Says:</u>

"I have no will power and yet I tend to achieve more than most."

I am all or nothing. I steamroll the world or sleep my life away. I have unlimited discipline or no discipline.

For example, I like to eat. Counting out calories for six evenly space meals simply presents six separate opportunities for me to overeat. Hence I do intermittent fasting.

By using IF, I only eat twice each day. I can eat large meals. Because I fast for 16-18 hours out of the day, I am not tempted to overeat.

Likewise, I don't bring junk food into the house. If there's junk food in front of me, I will eat everything. If there's no junk food in the house, I won't even walk across the street for it. Hence, no junk food is allowed in my home.

I eat with small dishes and small spoons. This places tricks on your mind. You think you're eating more than you actually are.

At the gym, I don't count reps or sets. I have no plan going into the gym. Sure, I don't look like a *Men's Health* cover model, but my physique and level of athleticism are higher than most. I do posture exercises all day, because science shows that dominant behavior and posture increase your testosterone level.

I wear the same outfit each day. I have several pairs of gym pants from Gold's Gym in Venice and several different colored Henleys. I either wear gym pants and a Henley or blue jeans and a Henley. I do not spend any time thinking about what I am going to wear.

I also don't fight myself. I'm honest and unapologetic about what who I am and want I want.

Because my brain is not wasting time on stupid decisions and because my life is not a lie, my brain has the energy it needs to hit it hard. *Danger & Play* exists in its present form because I don't spend hours a day worrying about nonsense like packing food, counting calories, counting reps in the gym, picking out a cool outfit, etc.

Dr. Jeremy Says:

"Mike is actually planning and making shrewd use of his limited resources."

Mike is doing a lot more to achieve his success than it appears at first glance. By projecting into the future and planning in small ways (like with fasting, not buying junk food, and using small spoons), he is able to act in the moment for greater progress with less stress. Here is the psychology behind how he does it…

As opposed to animals (like lizards) that primarily live in the moment, we have an added component to our consciousness called Symbolic Self Awareness (Sedikides & Skowronski, 1997). That added awareness allows us to imagine future behaviors and their possible outcomes (like buying snacks at the store), before we actually act them out in real life (and pig out at home). Essentially, it makes such future projections, plans, and goal-setting possible on a cognitive level.

As a result of this added symbolic awareness, we have the ability to improve ourselves by bouncing back and forth between setting future goals and immersing ourselves in present actions to reach those goals. This behavior has been described as a discrepancy-reducing feedback loop, also known as a test-operate-test-exit loop (Carver & Scheier, 1982). In essence, we project into an imagined future to set goals and plan (the test). We then perform behaviors in the present to get closer to those desired goals (operate). After a period of time, we compare the present to the future, in order to monitor our progress toward that future goal again (test). Finally, we either adjust and behave again (operate), or reach our set goal (exit).

This is the basics for why we flip-flop between present and future, in order to help us set and reach desired goals, and improve ourselves. It is also what Mike basically does to set plans and then "coast" through his day. **HOW he (and we) accomplish these activities is a bit more complicated**...

To begin, an individual needs to project into the future and set a goal. Such goal setting is essential because goals are the "test" that all present action will be measured against. In Mike's world, it is the time he spends envisioning his ideal physique and deciding on the general steps and goals required to get there. Those goals, in turn, help to direct attention to goal-relevant activities, increase motivation, prolong effort, and aid in strategizing for future success (Locke & Latham, 2002). To best accomplish that goals should:

- **Be Specific**: so that an individual can clearly measure success (e.g. deciding to lose 20 pounds is better than just wanting to lose weight).

- **Be Challenging**: in order to improve motivation and satisfaction upon completion. However, it should also be achievable in order to avoid discouragement (e.g. setting a 20-pound goal instead of five, because it is still achievable, but would make a bigger difference).

- **Be Important**: to meeting the person's needs (e.g. losing weight to promote health AND attractiveness).

- **Provide Feedback**: to help the individual be aware when change in behavior is needed (e.g. weighing every week to determine weight loss or getting a DEXA scan every few months).

Next, it is important to motivate the behaviors required to reach the goal. We "perform" in the moment by being propelled by two general types of motivation (Ryan & Deci, 2000). We may perform because of personal desires, needs, or values internal to ourselves (intrinsic motivation). We may also take action to obtain some sort of external reward, favor, or relationship (extrinsic motivation).

Although both types of motivation serve the same function, when possible, it is often better to set goals and perform behaviors that are at least congruent with intrinsic motivations and personal needs. That is why people who work "doing what they love" are often more satisfied and productive than those who work "for a paycheck." It is also why Mike says that he doesn't fight himself, and is true to who he is and what he wants. He is being congruent with his intrinsic motivations and using them to drive his behavior.

To stay on track, self-control is important. Staying in the moment, keeping focused, and persisting is not always easy. That is where discipline and self-control come into play. However, self-control tends to operate like a muscle, getting fatigued with repeated use (Muraven & Baumeister, 2000). Therefore, try to juggle too many tasks in a day and you're bound to let one slip. Fortunately, also like a muscle, self-control gets stronger after repeated exertion and rest.

Thus, to perform in the moment and reach goals, self-control needs to be used judiciously. Ideally, goals and behaviors should be staggered, to give times for rest and recovery. New endeavors should be added one-at-a-time. If that is not possible, then sometimes certain taxing behaviors or routines could be made more automatic and effortless with practice (Bargh & Chartrand, 1999). At other times, perhaps a change in general mood or reframing the task might make it less taxing; it's called emotion-focused coping (Lazarus & Folkman, 1984).

This is the area where Mike really shines. He streamlines many of his tasks to make them automatic. He keeps a positive focus, reducing stress and making things feel less like "work." In short, he makes careful use of his limited self-control to maximize success.

Finally, it is important to "test" again and adjust behaviors as necessary to reach goals. That is where the idea of implementation intentions comes into play (Gollwitzer, 1999). In short, implementation intentions are quick "If X, then Y" statements that lead to behavior prompts, much like conditioned reflexes or NLP anchors.

For example, if Mike sets certain times to fast, looking at the clock will automatically remind him about his diet (and not to eat yet). Similarly, if he associates certain dominant behaviors with the gym environment, those stimuli will prompt him to "hit it hard" when he walks in. Like Mike, by setting and conditioning these prompts, we can create little behavioral reminders that either keep us on track or help us change focus.

Overall then, looking into the future to plan and acting in the moment are two sides to the same coin of self-development. Switching between those states helps us to set goals, find motivation, control ourselves, and implement positive behaviors. Like with Mike, a little forethought also helps to reduce the clutter in our lives, reduce stress, and find greater success.

Now that you've read my thorough analysis of the mechanisms behind Mike's success… take one more cue from him: spend a few minutes setting a goal, then get off of your computer and go do it!

About Dr. Jeremy:

Jeremy Nicholson is a Social and Personality Psychologist, with a research and writing focus on influence, persuasion, dating, and relationships. He also holds master's degrees in Industrial/Organizational Psychology and Social Work. Dr. Nicholson shares his advice as a dating/relationship expert as the Attraction Doctor on *Psychology Today.*

References:

• Bargh, J.A., & Chartrand, T.L. (1999). The unbearable automaticity of being. American Psychologist, 54(7), 462-479.

• Carver, C.S., & Scheier, M.F. (1982). Control theory: A useful conceptual framework for personality-social, clinical and health psychology. Psychological Bulletin, 92(1), 111-135.

• Gollwitzer, P.M. (1999). Implementation intentions: Strong effects of simple plans. American Psychologist, 54, 493-503.

• Lazarus, R.S., & Folkman, S. (1984). Stress, Appraisal and Coping. New York: Springer.

• Locke, E.A. & Latham, G.P. (2002). Building a practically useful theory of goal setting and task motivation: A 35-year odyssey. American Psychologist, 57(9) 705-717.

• Muraven, M., & Baumeister, R. (2000). Self-regulation and depletion of limited resources: Does self-control resemble a muscle? Psychological Bulletin, 126(2), 247-259.

- Ryan, R.M. & Deci, E.L. (2000). Self-determination theory and the facilitation of intrinsic motivation, social development and well-being. American Psychologist, 55(1), 68-78.
- Sedikides, C., & Skowronski, J.J. (1997). The symbolic self in evolutionary context. Personality and Social Psychology Review, 1(1), 80-102.

What's Your 5-Year Plan? Your 10-Year Plan?

Have a seat, son, and let's talk about your goals. You might be 18 or 28 or 48. Your age doesn't matter. We need to sit down and talk, because if you fail to plan, you plan to fail.

Where do you see yourself in five years? Ten years? What are your goals?

It all seems overwhelming, and that's because your unconscious mind realizes something that none of these idiots talking about goals do.

Planning is for cowards.

People make plans for one reason only. They are cowards unwilling to accept that life is chaos and warfare.

They are cowards afraid of recognizing that success or failure depends upon outside circumstances that can be "planned around."

They are cowards unwilling to admit one undeniable and horrifying fact.

You are in control of you.

This is a horrifying realization because it means you must take personal responsibility for your life.

This is terrifying because you want an excuse to lose control of your thoughts, feelings, and emotions.

You want to rant and rave against the world and forces outside of your own control rather than take control over yourself.

You are afraid because once you accept that you are in control of you, then you cannot blame external circumstances or the "unfairness of life" for your station in life.

You don't have the courage to ask, "What is living life with no excuses like?"

I was once a coward.

It's 2014. Ten years ago I was about to graduate from law school.

Up until that time, I was an all-American boy. I was an officer in the Army Reserves. I worked my way through college. I followed all of society's rules.

I did everything right.

I planned on having a nice life. I was going to be a highly successful trial lawyer.

Then, as the cowards say, *"It was all taken from me."*

I got charged with rape. I was too stressed out to study. I lost my scholarship.

I cried myself to sleep and contemplated suicide.

"This is so unfair. It's not my fault! Why is this happening to me?"

Nothing was taken from me.

Nothing was happening to me.

I was happening to me.

I lost control of my life. That was a choice I made.

I choose to look outward at the cold, cruel world rather than inward at myself.

What was happening to me? *Me.*

What is happening to you? *You.*

Your only plan is *you.*

You don't know where you will be or who you will be with.

The only person you know will be there for you is you.

Your only answer to that stupid question about your five year plan is, "Me."

"What's your 5 year plan, Mike?"

Me.

"That doesn't make any sense, Mike."

It doesn't have to make sense to you. It's my life and only has to make sense to me.

Invest in yourself. YOU, Inc.

The only plan that ever worked in the history of man is for you to be the best man you can be.

Being the best or the worst or settling for mediocrity is a choice you make every day, and every minute of every day.

Life has hit you hard? Join the club, buddy. There's room to your right and your left, but it's going to be a tight fit. We could fill 10,000 stadiums with people who have been worked over by life.

We couldn't fill a single stadium with men who say, "Bring it on. Bring it *all* on."

"What, if some day or night a demon were to steal after you into your loneliest loneliness and say to you: 'This life as you now live it and have lived it, you will have to live once more and innumerable times more...' Would you not throw yourself down and gnash your teeth and curse the demon who spoke thus? Or have you once experienced a tremendous moment when you would have answered him: 'You are a god and never have I heard anything more divine.'"

Nietzsche, The Gay Science, §341.

Start planning now.

What are you going to do today to invest in yourself?

I walked my dog. He ran some sprints and is laying by my feet as I type this. I never touched my iPhone and gave him my full attention. If I had children, I would have spent my morning playing with them. Not iPhoning it in as a dad.

I talked to my consultant at BADNET about logo design.

I chugged a nootropic and talked with my business partner in that venture about product formulations.

I worked with my new web guy. (You've probably noticed some changes and may have gotten a PDF from me; sorry about that typo in there.)

I watched a Jeff Walker video and got a great idea. I'm going to convert a wall into a white board that you can write on and erase.

I'm going to the gym to jump rope and hit the heavy bag.

I'll do 100 or 1,000 small tasks that will build the road that I walk through life.

I'll be laying bricks for another 12 hours before sleeping like a man who has done something with his Sunday.

What are you going to do?

Are you going to sit around and rant about the unfairness of the world, like some Tumblr dork?

Play some video games?

Maybe you're getting over a hang over? "Ugh, my head hurts so much. I'll never do that again." (And then you take another drink.)

Jerk off to Internet porn like some filthy drug addict?

Are you going to cry yourself to sleep like some lovesick teenager?

Or are you going to make the decision to take ownership of your life?

Vigilance is a virtue you live every second of every day.

Vigilance is chief of the masculine virtues.

This post is on its ~~44th~~ ~~58th~~ ~~87th~~ 93rd edit. You'll still find a typo in it. The work is never done.

You make hundreds or thousands of decisions every day to win or lose, to conquer or retreat, to laugh or cry.

Each of these decisions is a brick you lay. Rome was not built in a day. Nor will your life be built in one day.

Start laying some bricks.

How to Get Out of Your Own Head

How can you get outside of your own head and live in the present moment? That's not a rhetorical question. How do you get outside of your own head?

I give my answer (along with some state control exercises) in the latest Danger & Play podcast.

<u>WARNING</u>: This is some esoteric stuff. If you approach this with a closed or negative mind, it will sound like nonsense.

If you actually apply the exercises to your own life, you will be able to get out of your own head.

Click play or find it on SoundCloud or iTunes. And while you're at iTunes, be sure to give me a rating or review. We are blowing up in the ratings, with 67 ratings and 42 reviews. Every review brings us all closer to creating a real community of like-minded men. Or read the transcript below.

<u>Show notes</u>:

- Go somewhere big to remind yourself of your own smallness.
- Big places include the ocean, mountains, or a Zen Garden.
- You can also listen to house music, self-hypnosis DVDs, or buy a Zen waterfall.
- Perceive rather than judge.
- Use all of your available senses: see the ocean, smell the ocean, taste the salt that is floating in the air, feel the sand on your skin, hear the waves crash.
- Once you have released oxytocin and serotonin into your brain, pause.
- Hold that state. Reflect on how your body feels.

• Then transfer that state of being in the present moment to everyday experiences.

Danger & Play Podcast #048 Transcript: How to Get Out of Your Head

And we are back, welcome. This is Mike Cernovich from *Danger & Play* and today we're going to talk about how to get out of your head, how to be in the present moment, how to be more engaged with the world and to not stand around and get lost on your own thoughts.

This podcast comes from a reader question and the reader question goes:

"I have a question. How would I get out of my own head? Sometimes I find it difficult to stop thinking about stuff and just be present in the moment. Even when I know I'm foggy and even when I know I'm not in the moment it feels like my mind just spirals out of control when I think about not being in the moment."

It's a great question and it takes a lot of work to learn how to be in the present moment. And the best way to learn how to be in the present moment is to practice being around big things. Then you take the state control podcast and you learn how to change your state when you are around small things.

Be around big things.

Have you ever been to a Zen garden? Have you ever wondered why is it that flowing water calms the mind?

Why is it that when you're at the ocean and you're on the sand and you hear the waves crashing in, it's very mellowing? Why is it that thunderstorms and big bold storms can be soothing and actually help you sleep sometimes? Why is it that there's a metaphor that philosophers use where they talk about going to the mountains or going into the wilderness?

My answer is that you need to be around big things to realize how small you are.

The problem that we all have is that we only live in our own minds and we only know and understand our own consciousness.

There's an experiment in the philosophy of consciousness which goes "How do you know that anyone else has consciousness?" I know I have consciousness because I can perceive my consciousness or I can kind of see my consciousness but that becomes sort of recursive doesn't it? How do you see your own consciousness? What is consciousness?

How do I know that you have a conscious mind? I can watch you and observe you and see you doing things that seem consistent, but how do I know you're not just zombies? Or how do I know you're not characters in a video game and that I'm the only one who has consciousness and that everyone else is just an automaton?

A philosopher of language who talked about consciousness, Wittgenstein, he called it the beetle in the box metaphor. Your consciousness is like a beetle and you see this beetle in a box. You know this beetle exists, but you can't see the beetle in anyone else's box. You can only see your own beetle. So because of that it's hard to get out of your own head because that is your existence. That is all that you base your existence on.

But when you go out in the ocean or you go into the mountains and you hear the thunderstorm and you just lay down there you can get out of your head because you're completely humbled.

That's why surfing (although I don't surf), surfing is so Zen for people. You're completely reminded of how small and insignificant you are and that there's a huge world outside of yourself. And then you just sort of start flowing.

So an exercise that I do is, I live by the beach so I walk to the ocean when I feel like I've been in my head a little bit too much and I'm starting to go a little bit too crazy. Maybe I bring a green juice, maybe I don't. And I just lay down, I like the sunset especially. And I just lay on the beach next to the ocean far enough away that the waves aren't going to crash on me and I do it at a time where I'm not going to get a horrific sunburn. And I just lay back, stretch my arms out, and spread my feet apart (almost like you'd do a snow angel).

If you kids have never grown up in the Midwest or in a cold climate, maybe you've never seen snow but, Google "snow angel," and kind of how you get your body. You just completely spread out. And instead of thinking, "How do I get out of my head?" You just listen to the water. Just listen to it. That's all you're doing, is you're starting to perceive it and you're starting to become consciously aware of the waves crashing in. Maybe you open your eyes and see the seagulls flying. And then you kind of see the sky and you see the colors in the sky start to change because we're approaching sunset and you see the blues and the purples and the yellows.

And you just focus on that and listen to that and then eventually you're going to get out of your head.

Because why?

I don't know why.

I remember the first time I saw the mountains; it made me believe in God because I said "Wow these mountains are beautiful," and think I thought "Well, everybody would think the mountains are beautiful right?" There's something about us. There's something about our DNA that makes us view mountains as beautiful and spectacular. And that makes us view water and other things as spectacular.

And that makes us view the universe and that looking out into the universe and the stars. There's something inside of us in our DNA and I don't understand it. I don't fully comprehend it. I'm not here to tell you whether God exists or what kind of god exists. But there is something universal in all of us that make us see things as majestic, bold, and sublime. And that gets us out of our heads.

Again, this is a mystery. Maybe you guys understand it and why we are that way. So that's how you start getting out of your own head. And then what you do is (this goes back to the state control) once you get out of your head, you start to "pin" that feeling into your body.

So let's say I'm on the water and the waves are coming in and I'm smelling the salt and I hear the seagulls. I see the seagulls. All I'm doing is perceiving. I'm not judging. Perceiving not judging. I'm not saying "What if this seagull takes a shit and the shit lands on my head? Or, I wonder if this water's polluted? Should I really be lying on this sand? Is the sand clean? What if a sand crab bites me?"

You are just perceiving everything. And when you get with something so big and so much bigger than you, you're able to just take it all in. And then once you sort of reach that state where you feel like you're not inside of your head… this is going to seem contradictory like so many things that I talk about but you have to go do it… if you just try to apply your Western logical mind to you're just going to say, "Well this doesn't make sense because he's about to tell me to get inside my own head." But when you do it, you realize that's not what you're doing.

So you're perceiving, taking it all in. Perceiving not judging.

And then all of a sudden your body and your physiology is going to change and you're going to feel, maybe some sort of elation. You might feel some sort of connectedness. You might feel very spiritual. You might feel an overwhelming sense of love or an overwhelming sense of compassion or an overwhelming sense of surrender. I can't tell you what you're going to feel, but I know what I personally feel.

I tend to personally feel more connected to other people and more connected to my work and the art that I do at *Danger & Play*. And one reason why I've been able to open up more to you guys is because I've learned how to perceive and not judge. Because when you perceive and not judge, that includes not judging yourself. That means I can open up more. I feel more connected to people. I almost feel like I have to tell this story.

Some of the ideas that I have for posts are things that maybe I would have been afraid to talk about or pictures of my skin and that struggle I had and how horrific that was. You know, people could take those pictures and make fun of me on the Internet, mock me, and there's a lot of mischief people could make with that. When you post your pictures online, you lose control of the message and people can do whatever they want to do and there are a lot of bad and mean-spirited people out there. So a lot of things we don't do is because were afraid, "What if people judge us?"

That's because we're judging ourselves, so when you get into this big vast expansive situation with mountains, water, or you could even get a self-hypnosis DVD or white noise. You could even get a water fountain for your own house. Actually, the coffee shop I'm about to head to has a no cell phone policy and it's practically a miniature Zen garden.

There's a waterfall and that water just becomes very hypnotic and very trance-like.

And another thing I do to get out of my head is I listen to certain house music, especially certain types of trance music. And then when I do that, really powerful trance music, like I've mentioned Above and Beyond and I've listed a few of my songs… really powerful music will take you over if you surrender to the process. Let it take you on the ride that your brain is going to go on. Just take the ride. Or as Hunter S. Thompson said about drugs, "Buy the ticket, take the ride."

I'm not advocating drug use or anything like that but that's what you're doing: buy the ticket, take the ride. Go to the ocean and just do it. Don't think about it. Don't nitpick my arguments and say, "Well, Mike said to get out of your head and go to the ocean, and then he tells you to perceive the ocean and not judge it, but then right as you start to feel it and perceive it he tells you to start thinking about it and channeling this. Well, that's completely illogical. I've just completely refuted his argument."

No guys, you think that I'm not a logical person and don't understand that? But another way to get out of your head too is that experience isn't always consistent with what we consider to be Western logic.

Because again, right, I just shredded my own argument. You guys are smart; you can just shred my arguments. But if you just go out and do what I'm suggesting you're going to say, "Whoa, okay. That does make sense. What he told me to do seemed contradictory but it's not." Then you start to appreciate the value of paradoxes.

And that's another way you start to get out of your own head, is if you read Zen riddles or Zen paradoxes. If you try to apply a logical mind to it you just get stuck in your own head and you just don't appreciate it. But then when you learn to appreciate paradoxes for what they are, suddenly you're able to get out of your own head. So again, get a self-hypnosis DVD, some kind of white noise or water noise, whale songs. I'm sure there's a bunch of different products on the market, if you guys know of any great products let me know.

If you live by the water, go to the water. If you live in the mountains, go to the mountains. Just go somewhere and listen to house music. Go somewhere where there's something just so big and so overwhelming that you have to take in the sensory experiences and then you stop judging.

OK, now you've stopped judging. And you start to feel that elation. It's almost drug-like. A guy that I'm friends with, *30 Days to X*, sort of talked about how he's able to create an oxytocin overload in his body and I said "Yeah I'm able to do that too, we'll do a podcast." Man, it's hard to explain. But you start to feel oxytocin, serotonin... I don't know what neurotransmitters. Again, I don't even fully understand a lot of this stuff.

And when you have that feeling inside of you, that feeling that you're connected and that you're perceiving not judging then get back inside your body. "What do I feel like? Where do I feel these feelings? Do I feel it in my arms, my hands, or my brain?" It doesn't matter where you feel it. You might feel it in your erogenous zones; there's no wrong answer because you're still in perception mode. And you start to pin this now. Pin this feeling into you.

"Okay, this is how I feel when I'm not in my head." And then you do that repetitiously. Do it again on the beach. Do it again. Do it every day. Do it as many times as you can throughout the day. Do it as many times as you can throughout the week. The important thing is that you just start doing it. And then suddenly, once you've been able to pin these feelings to a certain experience, then you're able to reverse engineer it.

So right now, I'm making myself not be inside my own head. How am I doing it?

Either consciously or unconsciously to change my physiology, and I'm changing my physiology to feel the same way I feel when I'm at the ocean.

So even though I'm not at the ocean, I'm able to feel that way as if I'm there. Granted, it won't be quite as powerful as when you are there, but it's still a very powerful feeling. And then suddenly, you're not in your own head. You're not thinking, not judging, and your brain isn't spiraling out of control. You just become in the moment and you become very Zen.

And this is all active meditation. I'm not sitting in a corner in the lotus position OMing to a gong. I'm actively meditating and actively engaged in my life, that's how I do it. Does that make sense?

This might sound esoteric, if it doesn't make any sense, just go do it. If you go do it, it will make complete and total sense.

If you just read the words on the screen and you think, "Ehh makes sense (or not)," it's not going to make sense.

You have to actually do it, and when you do it, that's how you get out of your own head.

Thanks for tuning in.

How to Attract Anything You Want with the Law of Attraction

In life, nothing is freely given to you. You must take what you want. You can get anything you want in life—money, a muscular body, girls, friends—if you follow this three-step process.

Click play or go to SoundCloud to find out more. Also, you can subscribe via iTunes. If you're on iTunes, please rate the podcast. It helps the podcast move up in the algorithms and ensures that our message reaches even more men.

The law of attraction is thought of as hokey pokey, "The Secret" nonsense where you send energy out into the universe and it comes back.

Although there is some truth to that, there's a better way to think of the law of attraction.

The law of attraction is thinking about something in a conscious way because that will direct your unconscious mind to seek out those opportunities. In other words, your unconscious mind is going to start attracting, like a magnet, the things that you want.

I'm going to use myself as an example which I hate doing, but if you guys start sending me stories, I'll start using your stuff as an example.

So we'll talk about a little bit about me, but this is all about how you can use the law of attraction for yourself. So every month since December, *Danger & Play's* traffic has gone up.

And the reason it's gone up is because I thought, okay, I want to hit a certain number. And that was what I was attracting. That is what I was meditating on, that is what I wanted. So I hit that number really early and I thought, "Okay, I want to hit another number." And I hit that number. And then I decided, "Okay, every month I'm going to get a higher traffic number and then I'll probably peak or plateau."

I thought I plateaued last month, and then… no. I'm actually a little bit higher this month than I was last month. Now think about this. We are talking about this in June. May has 31 days and June only has 30 days. We have 2.5 days left in the month. I decided I wanted to hit a different number, which would be a twelve percent increase over what I hit last month.

And remember we are a day short and that growth every month is, generally speaking, unsustainable. So how did I start attracting all this traffic? When you meditate on what you want and you visualize what you want, you start seeing opportunities everywhere.

And here's where people go wrong: when you see the opportunities you have to take them.

That's what people don't do. People will meditate on or say "I want to make $100,000 this year or I want a 6 figure income." And then they see opportunities and they don't take them. There was this lunatic guy, Elliot Rodger and he read about the law of attraction, and he said "I meditated on winning the lottery," or something like that, which doesn't require you to take any action other than the empty gesture of buying a lottery ticket.

And he said, "I want to attract girls." And then he didn't meet all these girls. If you read his actual autobiography or his manifesto, you would see that there were girls everywhere. There were opportunities everywhere, but he didn't take them.

This is how the law of attraction really works:

Step 1. You focus on your vision, what you want.
Step 2. You are going to see opportunities everywhere.
Step 3. Seize the opportunity. You take what you want. You keep what you kill.

Here's an example.

Step 1. Last night I was thinking, "I would really like to hit that twelve percent increase in traffic." Suddenly, a post came to mind: "Who Do You Think You Are?"

It was a really cool post that you guys liked. I sent an email out and people loved it. The response was overwhelming. In fact, I got a bunch of emails that I have to sort through and it was fantastic. That came to me, that opportunity came to me because I meditated on my desired outcome.

Step 2. I had to see the opportunity or find the opportunity.

Step 3. Seize the opportunity. Take what is mine.

The same thing happened today. I was thinking, "Man, can I hit this traffic goal? Can I hit it? No, it's a Saturday. Saturday and Sunday are the worst days of the week for traffic. If you hit a real homerun on Monday, you might come close, but you're not going to hit it."

And then I just thought and thought.

I was at this meeting called METAL, which stands for Media, Entertainment, Technology Alpha Leaders. It's a pretty cool group. Then it hit me.

"Whoa whoa whoa, wait a minute. There are all these amazing speakers on stage right now talking about cool things that the people who read *Danger & Play* would love to learn about, but they don't have the opportunity to learn because they live across the country. Maybe they live in an area where there isn't a lot of technology concentration. Why don't you just write notes? Why don't you just take notes on what these people are saying on your iPhone, and then when you get home, write it up? Wouldn't that be amazing?"

That would be great for me because taking notes would make me internalize the message better. It would make me pay attention better instead of Tweeting people or whatever.

It would be great for readers, as you can learn something.

I would be focused more on that and I could deliver value and goodwill to *Danger & Play* readers.

And BOOM!

I had another post.

That I never would have had the idea for that METAL post if I hadn't been meditating and attracting that traffic goal that I wanted to hit.

It's not enough just to think, "Oh, I want to hit this traffic goal. Oh, I want this six-figure income. Oh, I want to meet this girl."

You have to meditate on that, yes. Because meditating is going to what? Allow you to SEE the opportunity. S-E-E the opportunity. Then seize the opportunity.

If I had said "Oh, I want to hit this traffic goal. Wow, these amazing speakers are on. One of these speakers was an early investor in Facebook. He organized all these major worldwide concert events. He traveled with the Rolling Stones. He runs a huge fund. Another guy talked about self-publishing."

I could have said, "Oh, that's nice. I guess I could write about it. La-de-de, la-de-da." If I didn't seize it though, if I didn't take the notes, and go home right away and write it all out, I wouldn't get it done, right?

Now, why am I doing this podcast? Let's get a little bit meta. I'm talking about the law of attraction and how I used the law of attraction to get traffic. And what is this podcast going to do? It's going to get listens.

I'm going to drop this at midnight or maybe tomorrow morning (this is Saturday) and BOOM. Again, I have a whole other post that is useful to you. This is information you may can use and apply to your life immediately.

And the podcast (and transcript) will bring me closer to the traffic number I am attracting.

And it just sort of came to me like it was magic. Again, because my unconscious mind is keyed in to opportunities in ways that it wasn't six months ago.

Let's talk about money. Right now, I'm not meditating on attracting money. I'm meditating on attracting readers, readership, and getting the readers engaged, and getting you guys just meeting each other. That's the vision for now. But money is already trickling in without me even trying to attract it.

And without even looking deeply, I am seeing money everywhere. "Whoa, I could do a whole marketing course based on what I learned." I could give a whole course on how to do a podcast, how I got my podcast on iTunes, why my podcast has more ratings than James Altucher's *Ask Altucher*, and what have I learned about social media marketing (what works and what doesn't).

So I have all these income rivers that could be coming in, right? That I'm not even trying to attract now. But the opportunities are already there. I'm already hearing from people about stuff that we could do, collaboration that we could do.

You must become obsessed to the point of madness.

Remember that post? Become obsessed to the point of madness. Meditate on what you want. Visualize it. Feel it.

Whether it's six-pack abs, whether it's a muscular body, or maybe you were in a car accident and just getting out of bed is going to hurt. Or maybe you're in a wheelchair and you feel depressed and despondent, and you don't feel like life has been fair to you. Or maybe your parents got divorced, or maybe you're in high school with really bad acne.

I don't know what you're going through, but I know you're going through something. I know that you want more out of life than what you have.

I know that you want to go from average to alpha.

Again, here's what you need to do:

1. Visualize. Meditate.

And what I mean by meditate is to actively think, "This is what I want to do."

2. See yourself doing it. Begin noticing opportunities.

If you are thinking about that six-figure income, think about that check. And what's going to happen is, I promise you, you will start seeing opportunities everywhere.

Now when you see these opportunities, that's going to be the difference between winning and losing. Winner and losers. Normal people and people like you who are listening.

3. When you see the opportunities, you have to take them.

If you do that and follow that three-step process, I promise you that you will attract whatever you want out of life.

You Have Already Mastered Visualization

You can use visualization exercises to help you achieve anything from business success to meeting girls. Yet whenever I write or talk about visualization exercises, my inbox fills with questions: "How do I learn how to visualize success?"

That's an unfortunate question, as it shows the failings of our educational establishment. You have already mastered visualization.

Visualization only seems complicated. It's actually simple. In fact, you are already a master at visualization.

Do you think about the past?

Do you ponder bad memories?

When you think about the past, do you involve one or more of your five senses (sight, sound, taste, touch, smell)?

Do you feel happy or sad when you think about the past?

In other words, does thinking about the past elicit an emotional response; that is, does it change your state?

Of course!

Thinking about the past is nothing more than performing a visualization exercise.

What if you started from the proposition that your past does not exist? What if you treated memories are being no more real than imagination?

That view is not too far off base. There's a large body of cognitive science showing that our memories range from horribly biased to outright false.

When you think about the past—and this is especially true of negative or sad memories—you develop feelings of sadness, rage, bitterness, resentment, or disempowerment.

You feel this sadness because you **choose** to treat your memories as if they are real. Make no mistake: that is a choice you make in the present moment.

Your memories are real only because you choose to treat them as real.

What would happen if you treated your <u>dreams</u> as being more real than your memories?

Try it out.

For the rest of the day, do not think about the past. When a memory arises, remind yourself, "This is not real."

Instead of thinking about the past, daydream about the future.

Imagine what you want.

Involve all of your available senses.

Visualize your perfect day.

Treat this imagined perfect day as being real.

Use those visualization skills that you have wasted on thinking about the "past" to dream about a better future.

You'll be surprised by what (or who) you attract.

Frame Control: How to Turn Your Problems into a Source of Power

State—or mood—is how a person feels when facing an obstacle. There are exercises a person can do to change his state.

My experience shows that more cerebral and introverted types do not respond as well to "state change" therapy. By "more cerebral," I don't mean smarter. I mean that we tend to live inside of our heads.

Since we introverts live in our heads, we don't respond as well to exercises that change our emotions, as emotions tend to exist in the body. (Yes, I know that the mind-body connection is a false duality and that mind influences and body and vice versa. But some of us are *more* influenced by one than the other.)

What can we do?

Well, first, we need to understand what is going on. We need to deconstruct our negative emotions, to find the causal connections. A to B to C to D.

Then we need to intervene in the appropriate way at the appropriate time.

The Emotional Cascade
Thoughts >>>> Self-Talk (Frame) >>>> Emotions (State) >>>> Power

What are thoughts? Where do they come from? Do you *see* your thoughts or do you *hear* your thoughts?

I have no idea where my thoughts come from. I do know that thoughts have some origin, which is why I strictly control my environment to avoid negative people and losers.

I do know, however, that I hear my thoughts. My thoughts lead to self-talk, and I talk to myself non-stop. Some people wonder how I can write so much and not burn out. I have thousands of unwritten posts in my head.

The talk never ends. Sometimes it's stupid talk, sometimes it's smart talk. But the voice is always there. Until recently, I just never bothered to sit down and share the self-talk.

I am totally ruled by my mind and by thoughts of unknown origin that lead to self-talk.

Since I cannot understand where thoughts come from, I must intervene where I can: at the self-talk portion of the model. (If you see your thoughts, what is that like? Reach out to me.)

Let's find a way to help those who see their thoughts.

Reframe your problems.

Framing is how you mind perceives whatever situation you are in. Framing is how you choose to *think* about an issue.

Let's look at an example of framing by pondering a hypothetical question:

Would you rather win a silver medal or bronze medal?

The rational answer would be that silver is better than bronze. Duh, bro!

Yet the research shows that bronze medalists are actually happier (when all is said and done) than silver medalists. See *When Less is More: Counterfactual Thinking and Satisfaction among Olympic Medalists.*

*"Research on counterfactual thinking has shown that **people's emotional responses to events are influenced by their thoughts about "what might have been."** The authors extend these findings by documenting a familiar occasion in which those who are objectively better off nonetheless feel worse. In particular, an analysis of the*

emotional reactions of bronze and silver medalists at the 1992 Summer Olympics—both at the conclusion of their events and on the medal stand—indicates that bronze medalists tend to be happier than silver medalists. **The authors attribute these results to the fact that the most compelling counterfactual alternative for the silver medalist is winning the gold, whereas for the bronze medalist it is finishing without a medal.***"*

That's framing. A silver medalist frames the issue as, "I could have won the gold. Second place is first loser!"

A bronze medalist frames the issue as, "I could have not won a medal at all. Lucky me!"

Frame your problem as being small relative to a worse problem.

I know that we live in a world of narcissism where whatever problem you are facing is so freaking important and unique and unlike anything else. You poor dear!

The truth is that you need to get over yourself and stop focusing only on yourself.

I don't say that as a moralist. I say that because it's what's best for you.

You can watch YouTube videos of oppressed people accomplishing amazing things. There's a man on YouTube who has no arms and legs.

He has *real* problems.

Rather than sitting around crying or bugging his friends with his stupidity and seeking attention and validation, he has taken action and created the best life possible for himself.

Frame your problems relative to his.

Now how do you *feel* about your problems?

If you really think deeply and get over yourself, you feel less crappy.

You might even feel pathetic, saying, "My problems are nothing! It's time for me to take action and to change my life!"

Frame your problems as a source of power. Problems equal preparation for something great!

You have a problem. We all have problems. The only thing within our control is how we choose to think and feel about those problems.

Oftentimes, life throws adversity at us that we never would have chosen to endure.

What if you framed your problem as elite training that Special Forces soldiers undergo? What if you said:

"Once I've gotten through this problem, I will have a reservoir of strength that will make me unstoppable!"

You still have the problem. It is the same problem you had three seconds ago.

But notice how you're thinking about this problem.

You are choosing to think about this problem as a source of power. It is preparation for life.

When you're feeling miserable, you change your thought. "Yes, this hurts. This sucks. But once it's over, no one will be able to stop me."

Stop talking about mommy and daddy.

All of our parents screwed up raising us somehow. Whatever. Your mommy didn't love you? Or she loved you too much? Your daddy wasn't there? Or he was too strict?

You can think about that like a child or you can view your challenging childhood as a source of power.

Say what you will about Jordan Belfort's ethics, but the man has a point about how you should frame your past.

"You are not your past, you are the resources and capabilities you glean for it. That is the basis for all change. If you survived the worst of the worse and are still breathing, you can learn from that."

What would happen then? How would you view your problems?

Would you feel sorry for yourself? Would you be a sad little panda who needs some milk and cookies?

Or would you have the mindset of a conqueror even at the lowest point in your life?

Or would you feel like you were going through Boot Camp and that at the end you would be an elite soldier?

It all starts with a choice.

Yes, it is a choice.

You can choose how you feel by choosing how you think.

You can choose to view your problems as special and unique.

Or you can view your problems as being nothing compared to what others have endured.

You can choose to view your problems as pointless suffering.

Or you can choose to view your problems as preparation for life.

The choice, as always, is yours.

Motivation and Inspiration

Go Back to Basics

Although my writing has been productive, I haven't felt that magic, spark, or what Mihaly Csikszentmihalyi calls *Flow* (Amazon). I used to be able to do a podcast each day. Now I'm, as the kids say, "just not feeling it."

Fortunately, I know how to diagnose the problem. Chances are you have had a similar problem, even though you work in an entirely different field.

If you have hit a roadblock in your life, you need to do something simple.

Go back to basics.

"I'm a good shooter, but when I shoot poorly, I go back to the basics." – Army Ranger firearms instructor.

What puts you in a state of flow? It could be anything, such as checking in to become more mindful or performing a brain warm-up.

I know what puts me into flow, and I haven't been doing it. **For me, the recipe for massive productivity is simple.**
When working:

- Two to four hours alone.
- Headphones on.
- Coffee.
- Empty stomach.
- House Music (Rony Seikaly mixes are nice) playing.

When not working:

- Hard cardio (heart rate to 190 if possible).
- Sweat profusely.
- Sauna/steam room and/or contrast showers.
- Do not weigh more than 210 pounds.

- Wander around/walk alone.

(I like to bring myself close to death.)

Due to various changes in my life, I haven't had enough time alone. My brain hasn't been given the freedom it needs to run wild.

I also neglected to do cardio and got fat while some injuries healed.

I unconsciously put an artificial constraint on my creativity.

Would you believe me if I told you money is making me less creative? Well, it has!

The *Juice Power* books are selling nicely and should continue selling well. This should be great news, shouldn't it?

Before writing I have started to think, "How will this post make me money?" I did not want to write or podcast unless that post or podcast would make me money.

Don't get me wrong. Keep buying the juicing eBooks. They are great and I shook myself out of it.

Monetizing *Danger & Play* has reminded me to focus on my mindset, which is that I write whatever the fuck I want to write whether it makes me money or not.

If a post makes me money, great!

If a post makes you butthurt, you stop reading, and the post costs me money, great!

Ultimately, I do Danger & Play *for me*. Whatever happens, happens.

("No remorse, no apologies, no regrets.")

You can't skip the basics.

"We'll begin with the basics: the fundamentals. Trust me on this, now and for the rest of your Ranger careers, it will always be about the fundamentals: always. Refinements, yes, but always the fundamentals." – *Sua Sponte: The Forging of a Modern American Ranger*

We live in an instant gratification world. Life hackers tell you how to learn a foreign language and make millions of dollars in four hours a week!

Yet that is a lie. Even the life hackers selling you on easy money work brutally long hours.

You can't become a master until you've mastered the basics.

"Accident is ignorance, intention is style." – Phil Williams.

My high school English teacher would penalize students for bad grammar. One of the "monster errors" (comma splices, run-on sentence, subject-verb disagreement) would turn an "A" paper into a "C."

When students would complain, he would say, "You may use run-on sentences all you like. But if you accidentally use a run-on sentence, it's a monster error."

His point—which has stuck with me—is that rules matter when you are beginning any new endeavor. Do not begin a sentence with "and" until you understand what *and* is and how *and* is used.

"Accident is intention, intention is style," is a monster error known as the comma splice. But sometimes separating two independent clauses with a comma works better than separating those clauses with a period.

Indeed, Winston Churchill was a master at breaking rules of grammar, only because he knew them so damned well.

"We shall go on to the end. We shall fight in France, we shall fight on the seas and oceans, we shall fight with growing confidence and growing strength in the air, we shall defend our island, whatever the cost may be."

I don't know what your profession is, so I can't tell you how to master it.

I can give you the mindset tools you need.

First you need to make the Gorilla Mindset shift. No shortcuts. No life hacks. No easy way out.

Second, you need to discover what puts you in peak flow.

Start living an *intentional* life.

There is a way for you to reach flow, to become a stylist at life.

Don't judge why something puts you into peak flow or not. For example, I have sometimes watched porn before writing. When I'm especially horny, it doesn't help to have a raging hard-on while working. Even though porn is a filthy habit, sometimes it's a tool to give you a necessary release.

If watching porn or doing [insert "bad" habit] puts you into flow, why judge it?

Experiment. Jump rope, do jumping jacks, take a long walk, scream in an empty room, take a cold shower. I don't know what works for you, but there is something you can do that will work for you. I promise you that.

Maybe you felt especially awesome or on-point one day. That was an accident borne out of ignorance. Turn that accident into style.

Think about a time you felt unstoppable.

- Who were you with?
- What were you doing?
- When did you feel amazing?
- Where were you?
- Why did you reach flow?

You may even want to look into self-hypnosis. For example, I use this hypnotic pattern to improve my reading comprehension:

Notice the paper. What color is it? Notice how clean and crisp it seems. Fingers slide over the surface, and feel how smooth they are. Eyes can flow across the page, going easily from side to side, seeing everything.

Notice the letters on the page. They seem dark and distinct. The round parts of the O's and C's are very smooth; the up and down parts of the T's and L's are tall and strong.

The printing is especially vivid. The words seem to stand out very clearly.

Handbook of Hypnotic Suggestions and Metaphors (on Amazon).

Master the basics. Find your flow.

Have you mastered the basics?
What puts you in flow?

How to Survive Hell

"If you're going through hell, keep going." – Winston Churchill

It's a sunburn that won't heal. Your skin feels like it's on fire. Your whole body itches. It hurts to move.

You wake up. You can't get out of bed.

Your eyelids are swollen. You have to pry them open with your fingers because some sort of ooze has glued them shut.

Keep moving.

You take six steps towards your front door before leaning against the couch, out of breath.

"I'll just walk down the stairs and take the elevator up," you say.

Keep moving.

It's been another 18-hour day of clawing at your skin while your bones ache and your hair falls out.

You can't sleep. It's cold outside. Get out of bed.

Keep moving.

You look like a leper. You can't go out into public looking like this.

You don't care. Let them judge. It's not about them.

Keep moving.

Your hands are split open. Making a fist slices small cuts into your hand like an X-Acto knife.

Doesn't matter. Wrap those bitches up. Let them bleed into the gauze. Off to the gym.

Keep moving.

Self-doubt sets in. You tell yourself you're weak. Why bother going to the gym?

It doesn't matter if you're moving big weights. You're here, where you belong.

Keep moving.

You get out of your car. Lifting your chin up causes the skin around your neck to split open.

You feel sweat sting every inch of your body.

We don't have time to care about that.

Keep moving.

People ask how your skin is doing. You tell them that your skin is the least interesting topic to talk about.

They are curious and insist. You give a look. You don't have time to dwell on that.

You're too busy moving.

You're going to be in a private Hell.

If you can't walk, you crawl. If you can't crawl, you squirm. If you can't move, you blink. If you can't blink, you think.

There is only one way to survive Hell.

Keep moving.

Your Moment is Coming

You don't know when or where it will happen, but it will. Your day is coming.

That day could be a dream or a nightmare. You will experience riches beyond imagination or a crisis that sends you to hell.

Most people coast through life. They aren't ready when that moment hits them.

In our lifetimes, we may make millions of dollars, live the sex lives of Roman emperors, see our children graduate from Harvard.

Or we may get cancer. Our children may die in a car crash. I have seen it all, and when it happens, most are not ready.

Male suicide rates spike after divorce. A man's wife leaves him. Because the man was a beta supplicant without core values or a sense of what it means to be a man, he is crushed and kills himself.

All of those years kissing a woman's feet would have been better spent building himself up as a man, but most men (are you one of them?) are afraid of what they can become. They chose to lose themselves in someone else, to live a life of needy co-dependence.

Or maybe your *8 Mile* Moment approaches.

"You only get one shot, do not miss your chance to blow / This opportunity comes once in a lifetime yo." – Eminem

The person you always wanted to impress sees you, and he is not impressed. You were too busy goofing off to prepare for your moment.

Rather than hone your craft and become a master, you chose to live a life of needless distraction. (Or perhaps you put your full faith and credit into a relationship with someone other than yourself.)

Luck, as Seneca the Younger noted, is "the point where preparation meets opportunity." Your day arrives. You blow it. You blame "dumb luck."

Yes, dumb luck was involved, although the *dumb* is an adjective best describing the man.

You see an opportunity but you can't take it, for you were unprepared.

I have prepared all of my life for something. What that something is... I don't know.

"Mike, I need to meet with you right away," my friend at *Wall Street Playboys* said. "Why?" I asked him.

"You are about to become famous," was his reply. I laughed.

Sure enough, through no effort of my own, I started becoming famous. How? It just happened. Dumb luck, as they say.

Maybe my day has come.

I have been writing in one form or another for twenty years. Twenty fucking years. If you count my blog posts, journal entries, and forum posts, I have written several million words.

Twenty years and millions of words and people ask me why *Danger & Play* is so successful. As if there are any tricks.

I started getting recognized in public last year, and 2014 led to an insane interest in me and my work.

I prepared for this moment all of my life. I didn't know I was preparing for it. I didn't know when it would happen.

Yet it did.

Your moment will come. You will soar to a high-high or crash to a low-low.

Will you be ready when that day comes? What are you doing right now to prepare?

How to be at the Right Place at the Right Time

Arturo Sandoval is one of the world's greatest musicians. People fly across the world to watch him perform, and playing with him is considered a highlight of any musician's career.

When Sandoval was in town to perform, I was fortunate enough to attend his concert. While the show itself is a haze, something happened that I'll never forget.

Sandoval stepped off the stage for a brief intermission. His producer took the mic and told us a story that gives me chills to this day.

—–

"I had to stop by Nordstrom," Sandoval's producer began, "for some grooming stuff that I forget on the road."

"While walking down the block back towards my hotel, I heard a familiar sound. Someone was playing *Moon River*. I turned around and saw it was a young boy. I started to walk away, but something pulled me back towards him."

"I stood silently by while the boy continued playing. After he had finished, I told him that my father-in-law wrote the score for that song."

The child's eyes lit up.

"You know Henry Mancini?!" the boy exclaimed.

Impressed by his musical knowledge, the producer asked the boy whether he had ever heard of Arturo Sandoval. The child had and was excited to meet someone so famous, or at least someone who knew someone so famous!

The producer noticed something about the boy. He was playing on a used trumpet and clearly did not come from a family of means.

Even the cheap seats at the Sandoval concert would have been out of reach for the boy's family. So the producer invited the boy and his mother to attend the concert as Sandoval's special guest.

The boy impressed Sandoval, and the producer and Sandoval had a surprise for him.

Halfway through the show, Arturo Sandoval himself welcomed the boy to join him on stage. Together, they played *Moon River*.

—–

What losers will think.

The unmotivated will say that the child got lucky. He was at the right place at the right time and hit the lottery.

That is a loser's mindset that misses the real truth. Yes, the boy was at the right place at the right time. But it was no accident.

The boy was at the right place at the right time because he put himself there. He said the right things because he knew what to say.

The kid could have been playing video games, watching television or getting into trouble with his friends. He could have been wasting him time reading *Buzzfeed*.

He instead was doing something else: the only thing that mattered. He was mastering his craft.

Are you at the right place at the right time?

I left out the best part of the story. After playing together, Sandoval told the boy that he needed a better trumpet, and he handed the boy one of his own. This would be like Michael Jordan or Kobe Bryant giving a game-winning basketball to a teenage ball player.

Somewhere, an 11-year-old boy is playing a trumpet on an anonymous street corner.

What are you doing to be at the right place at the right time?

You Have Enough, You Are Enough: The Abundance Mentality

What is a mindset and why does mindset seem like such an abstract concept? The Oxford
English Dictionary defines mindset as "an established set of attitudes held by someone." Webster's says that mindset is "the ideas and attitudes with which a person approaches a situation, especially when these are seen as being difficult to alter."

That isn't much help, is it?

Mindset seems obtuse for good reason. We aren't taught to think about mindset. We are taught to follow rules.

Your entire life is based on following rules, on being a slave, on not thinking for yourself.

You were told in school that you were good or bad based on your grades.

Your parents said you were good or bad you based on whether you obeyed them, even if they were idiots and full of crap.

Society said you were good or bad based on how well you conformed to its expectations.

"Holy men" said you were good or bad based on whether you obeyed rules that they themselves refused to follow.

Mindset is different. Mindset is a choice about how you view reality.

https://soundcloud.com/dangerandplay/mindset-not-rules-abundance

What is the difference between a scarcity and abundance mentality?

The cause of anxiety and panic and many misunderstandings between people can be explained by a key difference in mindset: that of abundance and that of scarcity. A man with an abundance mentality believes, "I have enough," and, "I am enough." He looks at the value of relationships rather than the costs. The person with a scarcity mentality is always obsessed with counting nickels and dimes.

Neither approach is superior. Yet it's important to know what your mindset is.

A person with a scarcity mindset thinks of what things will cost. A person with an abundance mindset thinks of what he will attract.

Having a scarcity/abundance mindset doesn't make the person good or bad. People are different.

An abundance mindset does not mean you should be frivolous with money.

Wasting money is foolish, but money spent in the endeavor of making even more money is wise.

A man with an abundance mentality focuses less on what something costs and more about the value it will bring.

If your first thought is how much something costs, you might have a scarcity mentality. This scarcity mentality likely translates into all areas of your life.

You are enough and you have enough.

That doesn't mean you can't want more or shouldn't seek to find more.

But if you don't think you have enough and are enough today, when will you?

Will you have enough when you have $10 million? If you have a scarcity mindset, I guarantee that you won't.

I have been the guest of billionaires. You can be filthy rich yet not feel like you have enough. Will you feel like you are enough after you've slept with 100 women or received 100 gold stars? If you have a scarcity mindset, I promise that you won't feel fulfilled.

You are enough and you have enough.

Adopt an abundance mentality and soon you will have more money, more friends, and more relationships than you can handle.

Remember that like attracts like. If you are abundant, then you will attract other abundant people.

If you adopt a mindset of scarcity, then you will attract other like-minded people.

Who would you rather join forces with: self-possessed men with long-term vision and grand plans, or people who believe the world might end tomorrow?

You are enough and you have enough.

Be abundant.

What If?

What if failure does not exist, because life is not a test you are graded on?

What if rejection does not matter, because other people lack the power to make you feel small?

What if you give yourself permission to be weird?

What if you live your life with a sense of urgency and purpose?

What if you choose to stop living by their rules?

What if you stop blaming your parents, your culture, and your family?

What if you have the power to control how you think and feel?

What if you decide to take ownership and personal responsibility for your life?

What if you choose to live in a world of infinite resources and endless possibility?

What if everyday life is full of magic and wonder?

How will you live your life in that world of What If?

The Thin Line Between Breakthrough and Breakdown

"There's a thin line between a breakdown and a breakthrough, Rick. A very thin line." – Glow: The Autobiography of Rick James

I've learned through my own military and martial arts training—as well as studying elite soldiers—that we rarely push ourselves hard enough. When in doubt, push harder. When you feel like you can't take another step, you take 1,000 more.

You push through, but eventually something's gotta give.

Everything hurts. Moving hurts. Walking hurts. Lifting hurts. Standing hurts. Thinking hurts. Talking hurts. Writing hurts. Sleeping hurts.

I don't like taking no for an answer, so I keep moving.

Then I fall on my ass and have no choice but to rest.

I found my breaking point.

I started to break around the time of the New York meetup. Some of you commented that you heard exhaustion in my voice. I knew my body and mind were giving out on me and thus scheduled a vacation.

But I worked during my entire vacation and came back even more fatigued and beat up.

It's hard to stop pushing when you keep growing.

I have had ten months of consecutive growth on the website and the podcast. The *Danger & Play Podcast* is more highly rated than *Ask James Altucher*.

(The summer is a slow season and yet the site grows. September will be another record-breaking month.)

I'm launching an eBook.

I'm working on a nootropic.

I am working on a concept with a close friend that will offer some men a once-in-a-lifetime opportunity. We have no idea how the fuck we are going to pull it off, but we will.

And I'm broken.

What went wrong?

I should have stopped lifting weights.

Growing a business and growing your body violates the fundamental rule of Gorilla Focus, which provides, "A gorilla eats one banana at a time."

I could have dropped my training off to twice a week, maintained most of my muscle, and kept growing *Danger & Play*. But I broke my own rules, and then broke my own body.

I finally hit my breaking point doing box jumps.

I had had a small knot on my back. This created tightness on the left side of my body. Rather than wait until the knot was worked out, I insisted on training through it.

I missed the first jump, but refused to take no for an answer. Jump! Made it. As I went to stand up in triumph, my equilibrium shifted.

I'm sitting on my ass with a stinger on my left glute. The shock of the fall gave me a mild concussion. My instinct was to lay down.

I stand up.

"Oh shit," I think to myself, "I'm about to pass out." I can see stars and the rooftop where I train is spinning.

"Just take a few more steps. You can't fall down. Walk three more steps and then you can rest." I didn't pass out and I even jumped rope a bit in defiance of the injury.

Even so, now I have a knot in my back, a knot in my ass, and a sprained wrist.

As I type this post wearing a wrist brace, I feel that my Achilles is about to tear.

Muscle knots are one thing. An Achilles tear is something else. Time to chill.

"No regrets, no apologies, no remorse."

If you keep pushing yourself, you will eventually break. But there is beauty and majesty in destruction.

The harder you push, the stronger you get. The more you break down yourself, the stronger you build yourself back up.

We have been conditioned to believe that a breakdown is the end. A breakdown marks a new beginning. A breakdown offers a chance for what psychologist Kazimierz Dąbrowski calls positive disintegration.

What breaks you today will be your new baseline tomorrow.

Push hard. Recover harder.

When I get beat down, I use the recovery methods of professional athletes.

In the next part of this series, I'll talk about some of those methods.

Let's just say the pros have advanced well beyond the R.I.C.E. method.

Have you ever had a breakdown?

How to Survive a Crisis

What happens when the entire mainstream media attacks you in an attempt to ruin your reputation? Or what happens when you find yourself in any personal or professional crisis? Find out how you can survive any crisis the latest Danger & Play Podcast.

Treat Mediocrity as a Crisis

People are very good at doing two things: surviving crises and accepting mediocrity. To protect our egos, we use euphemisms for mediocrity. We say we are *good enough* rather than admit we have accepted mediocre life outcomes.

To some extent, we can blame evolution.

Our bodies are regulated by the parasympathetic and sympathetic nervous systems. As everyone learned in 9th grade biology, the parasympathetic nervous system is responsible for your bodily functions when you're at rest. You don't need willpower to breath, have a beating heart, or digest food. The parasympathetic nervous system puts us into "chill" mode.

Our sympathetic nervous system is responsible for the fight-or-flight response and gives us huge doses of adrenaline. If you heard a gunshot outside, your body would automatically give you a huge dose of epinephrine and norepinephrine. Your heart rate would skyrocket, your body would release glucose for fuel, and you'd be ready to move: to fight or to flee.

In other words, our bodies are evolved to help us avoid dying and to conserve energy. Our bodies are not evolved to drive us to accomplish great things.

Everyone has had to overcome some huge life crisis. We may smirk at a high school kid being emo about "having his heart broken," but when you put yourself into the shoes of a teenager, you remember how awful all that lovey-dovey shit was.

I would laugh at a guy with approach anxiety, and that would be unfair. There was a time when fear controlled my life, too. I am unsympathetic to the plight of newbies only because I live in denial of my former, weaker self. It is a character flaw that I am working on.

When life gets really bad, we find ways to overcome obstacles that seemed insurmountable. We find a way to make things happen. Yet we make things happen only when life forces us to.

Think about your last life crisis. You probably dealt with some huge problems. Your body became very stressed. You felt hopeless. Then somehow you were able to solve the problem.

You survived.

But you didn't rush to that crisis, did you? Instead, it was thrust upon you. You didn't have a choice. You had to either survive or die. You really didn't have a choice.

After surviving, you probably did what everyone else does. It's what society tells us to do. You went back to your normal life and waited for time to heal your wounds.

You did not take the resolve and fortitude you found deep within yourself and apply it to something else.

You didn't say, "Wow. I never thought I'd be able to solve that problem. Now that life is back to normal, I am going to use those same skills to take myself from a state of mediocrity to a state of excellence."

There are undoubtedly areas of your life that need work. You may suck at something and want to improve. Or you may be "good enough" but know you can become excellent.

If I put a gun to your head, could you accomplish your goals? Would you do something that you've been putting off? If I put a gun to your head, would anything stand between your current mediocre self and your excellent self?

What would happen to your life if you treated being mediocre not as something you can live with, but as a crisis that must be survived?

Zen and the Martial Art of Living

"For me, money has never been about buying things, it's been about freedom. That's my #1 value in life: freedom. And I'm always looking forward to the freedom that money can buy." – Nic Gabriel

Nicolas Gregoriades/Gabriel is a world-renowned BJJ black belt. Nic is famous for earning his BJJ black belt (under Roger Gracie, no less) in just over four years.

Lacking a home address, Nic travels around the world teaching Brazilian jiu-jitsu. He also operates a highly successful blog and podcast. He recently launched a clothing line. He earns his living doing what he loves.

Like you, Nic is on a quest to master himself and his emotions. You are going to love this.

Mike:

And we are back. This is Mike from DangerAndPlay.com and today I'm in the studio with...

Nic G:

Nicolas Gregoriades from JiuJitsuBrotherhood.com and TheJourneyPodcast.com

Mike:

So today is a really interesting and curious episode because it validates a lot of things that we talk about: the Law of Attraction and how you get the energy that you send out to the universe, and I'll explain why.

I remember it was two or three years ago where I watched this YouTube special on ayahuasca. And I saw this guy on the YouTube channel talking about his experience with ayahuasca, and I thought "Yeah, that's a cool guy, I'd like to meet that guy someday. He seems like he's insightful, introspective and he's on a quest. Cool guy. Maybe I'll meet him someday."

And then he moved on to other things so I lost track of the guy for several years and then a message forum that I read started talking about him, "Can you believe this article he wrote about performance-enhancing drugs? It seems like he's encouraging them."

And by encouraging them, they mean he didn't say that taking a shot of testosterone will immediately kill you. And I thought, "Oh wow, that's that same guy from way back when."

So as it turns out, I linked to his Ask Me Anything, and then he saw that I linked to it and then we started talking and he asked me where I live and I said "I live in Venice Beach." And he said, "No way! I'm in L.A."

And I thought, "Well, wow, that's kind of odd. So this guy that I saw three years ago who lived in London, happened to be in L.A. the exact day that I tweeted his AMA: that's quite a coincidence, isn't it?

Nic G:

Yeah I like to think so dude, and as you said, like attracts like.

I really love the way you said that "he's on a quest," because a good friend of mine many years ago he said... I think we were talking about *The Game* or something like that. He said that he met this guy and that he was a really cool guy and that he was "on the path," he's like us, he's on the path. And I thought that was a really cool way to describe someone who was making a concerted effort to improve themselves and increase their amount of joy, pleasure, and goodness in their life.

Mike:

So it's interesting because although Nick is a very well-known BJJ guy, I had never known him as a BJJ guy, so this isn't going to be another, "Oh, you trained with Roger Gracie? What was that like? What was it like being Roger Gracie's BJJ black belt?"

Although we will talk about some BJJ specific questions, we definitely want to go a little bit deeper than that. We want to talk about mindset, philosophy, and just your quest of how to find what you're looking for. How does that sound?

Nic G:

It sounds great man; I'm really looking forward to that.

Mike:

So why is it that you're in L.A. now?

Nic G:

Well, for those of you who don't know, I have a podcast called *The Journey* and the main reason I'm here is that I'm networking for that. There are a few people in this town that have really illustrious podcasting careers and they know how the industry works and there are also a bunch of jiu-jitsu industry players here that I have meetings setup with.

It's basically a networking trip primarily and secondarily, it's to relax and have a bit of a vacation because I really love the States and in particular Los Angeles.

Mike:

What made you decide to start a podcast?

Nic G:

Well, I had been involved in the London Real project for 14 or 15 months. And when the other co-creator and I went our separate ways, there were aspects of it that I missed, but I was so busy with my other projects that I didn't give it too much thought. And then a bunch of people started asking me, "When are you going to do your own thing?" or "When are you going to do another podcast?"

And I had someone I had started becoming friends with, a guy named Paul Moran and he had his own jiu-jitsu podcast that I had appeared on a few times before. And I think he might have brought it up, but strangely enough, I had been thinking the same thing. I thought, "This guy and I would make a pretty cool show if we did one today."

And one of us mentioned it to the other and before you knew it we had started our own show and it has gone on from there.

Mike:

Yeah, it really is pretty trippy that technology brings people today who never would have met 10, 20, or 30 years ago. So many guys think, "How do I meet like-minded men or how do I connect with people who see the world as I do?" And I think the biggest mistake that people make is expecting those connections to happen when you walk down the street. A lot of times, those connections are going to happen online.

Nic G:

Yeah. And you know there's that expression "You make your own luck."

This is a huge understanding which I've had recently, which is the Law of Attraction. I do believe there is some truth to it, but I strongly believe that the universe will only meet you half-way.

So if you sit on your couch and you say, "I want a million dollars," and you start thinking about a million dollars, there's no fucking way you're going to get a million dollars. It doesn't work like that.

But if you get off your ass and start moving toward what you want, then the universe takes notice and says "OK, I'll meet him halfway." That's the thing with technology; you can open up a Facebook account and expect people to connect with you or open up a Twitter and expect people to just start following you. But that's not how it works. You have to put in the effort and seek to engage with people and seek out the people you want to talk to and connect with.

Mike:

I think a lot of people misrepresent the Law of Attraction.

They say, "Oh, all you do is meditate on something and it's going to happen." But what happens is that when you start meditating on something, the transformative process happens within yourself. So if you say, "I want to start a podcast that gets a certain number of listeners," and you really meditate on that, then suddenly, something inside of you or outside of you, however you want to put it, kicks into gear and then it starts to push you into that direction.

Nic G:

I agree with you completely.

Also, you start to see the Law of Reflection in operation.

A guest on The Journey spoke about this. As you were saying, it's not necessarily that you attract everything in your own life; it's also that you reflect things in your own life. Well, the world is reflecting things back at you, so if I say to myself, "I want to start a super successful podcast," and then I'm focused on that, then I start seeing opportunities. The world starts reflecting opportunities back at me to do that as opposed to handing them to me on a plate.

Mike:

Exactly. You start to notice things that you never would have noticed. A classic example is, if you buy a Toyota Prius, you are going to look around and think, "Holy shit, there are Priuses all over the place." They were always there, but now you are noticing, or as you said, now you're reflecting. Now you see something that is always there, and the same is true of your thoughts.

When you get new thoughts in your head or buy a new thought so to speak, suddenly you're going to notice all those same people with those same thoughts.

Nic G:

Yeah. There's another interesting way to look at it which, Terrance McKenna is the person I believe I heard this from, and he was saying in a video of his called:

"Culture is your operating system."

The analogy is that your brain is like a piece of computer hardware and the culture in which you are raised is the software which the brain runs.

And he was saying how some of this software doesn't support specific plugins. So if you don't have a mind open enough to recognize certain things, you just won't see them. You literally won't even see them because your software is not supporting that. So for me personally, I'm always trying to upgrade my software and make it as flexible and open source as possible so that I can see these opportunities and choose whether to engage with them or not.

Mike:

It has always amazed me that people hold onto these views so strongly and are so confident that they are right and know what they are doing. And I'll ask them, well, "Where did you get these ideas?" Did you go up to Mount Sinai all by yourself and fast for 30 days, meditate and then come down with some stone tablets? And the answer is no.

Your culture, your society, your parents: they put all this stuff in your head, and even if there wasn't ill intention on their part, it's garbage. It's bad and it makes you engage in self-destructive behavior and it makes you come from a sense of powerlessness rather than from power. Part of the quest or the journey is putting new thoughts in your head or changing your software or however you want to put it.

Nic G:

Yeah, I have two thoughts on that come into my mind straight away. The first is that a lot of things society puts into your head are actually very good. Admittedly, a lot of them as you said are garbage, but I like the fact that I was programmed not to steal or not to fuck people over or just be, I don't want to say a "good" person but morals are a good programming thing up until a point.

Also, there was a point a few years ago of what I call the point where I was starting to wake up and I started to realize that I needed to literally analyze every single thought I had about everything. It's like, in the morning when I'd wake up and go to brush my teeth, I'd be like, "Well, why do I always pick up my toothbrush with my left hand or why do I brush my teeth in this way?" And I'd listen to my language and stock answers I'd give to people, and I'd be like, "Why do I always say that? Why do I always end the conversation with that phrase, etc.?" And it's just, for a long time I became very meticulous about my thought processes and my actions and then I could see which ones were coming from my instincts, I guess you could call it my soul, and which ones were things that had just been loaded up there. And then I could choose which ones to keep and which ones to do away with.

Mike:

That sounds really simple now, but let's talk about the panic and anxiety and self-doubt that occurs when you start to re-examine everything.

Nic G:

So, if you think about your psyche as a building with a foundation, you're going to go in there and take that foundation out and redo it. Obviously the structure is going to become wobbly and unstable. And that's what self-analysis is, or self-reflection is, especially when you go through that stage, it's like you have to take these supports that your whole life is based on and get rid of them.

That's definitely going to lead to anxiety and fear, but it's ultimately something you have to go through to have a bigger, stronger structure.

Mike:

Did you have a lot of anger or resentment toward any specific people as you went through this?

Nic G:

I mean, like my parents had a shitty marriage and they are always fighting and stuff, and yeah there was a lot of resentment and anger towards them. I had an issue with an ex-girlfriend. But ultimately, what a lot of that self-reflection showed me is that I was responsible for a lot of the things in my life.

And secondly, even the ones that I wasn't responsible for on a conscious level, the things that I thought were bad or horrible came with some hidden benefit that manifested at a later point and I was ultimately really thankful for them.

Mike:

Yeah, it's ultimately choice and how you perceive things, because no matter how you are raised or what your upbringing is, you can choose to view it negatively. "Oh well, I had too much money and because of that. I don't have hunger and I don't have drive," or, "I grew up poor and I was never provided opportunities that these other trust fund kids had." Or, "I never had this, I never had that." And the truth is that everyone was lacking in something in their upbringing or education.

Nic G:

Yeah, I completely agree with you. In fact, something that has become clear to me lately: my dad, he was a reasonably wealthy guy for a while, and then he lost everything. He took his eye off the ball, his business is fucked up, and he lost everything. I realized at one point that not only is there no more inheritance for me, but it's pretty likely that I'm going to have to support my parents into their old age.

At first, I was really pissed off about that and then I realized that this is a massive opportunity. If I had been some rich kid or some trustafarian, I might not have had that motivation. I might have just been content to sit around and do nothing with my life. And it made me really think that it was a blessing in disguise. That's pretty much the latest I've identified, but there are loads in my life. And I'm sure loads in the listeners' lives as well.

Mike:

Yeah, it really does come down to how you choose to frame what you have experienced.

You can frame it as an opportunity for growth, as an opportunity to learn, or you can frame it as victimization. "I'm a victim, I can't believe this happened." The trustafarian example is good because I know kids in L.A. that have multi-million dollar trusts and they sit around all day at a pool miserable and aimless. A few of them have died of drug overdoses. It's because they were given everything and because of that, they had no hunger for anything. And they hate their parents as much as anyone who grew up in an abusive environment.

Nic G:

Yeah. And what it comes down to for me is to ultimately start everything from, I was speaking about earlier about installing a new foundation. And I believe about that foundation is, one of the best ones you can have is gratitude. Be thankful for your life and its circumstances. Because it comes with its own set of challenges, opportunities, difficulties, and rewards that no one else's does.

I heard a saying a long time ago, I think it's a Chinese saying. I'm paraphrasing, it says:

"If every man were to bring his troubles and lay them out on a table in front of everyone else in the world, at the end of it he'd pick up his own troubles and leave with them."

We all have our own shit. And I guess, just be grateful for your circumstances right?

Mike:

Exactly. Everybody is dealing with something. That's the biggest thing that I've learned as I've gotten older. That millionaire that you're jealous of or that person that you covet is dealing with some problem.

Or you hear the joke, "Show me a hot chick and I'll show you a guy who's tired of putting up with her shit." No matter who you look at, somebody is dealing with something because we all ultimately only have our own consciousness to compare to.

I don't know what's going on in your head and you don't know what's going on in mine. And we can talk and communicate, but ultimately you have your thing and I have my thing and that's the blessing and the curse of being a human. And when you start to look at other people from a covetous nature, rather than being grateful for what you have, not only does that put you in a negative state of mind, but it's also delusion, because that other guy is dealing with all kinds of shit too.

Nic G:

Man I couldn't agree more. Big understanding for me. **Jealousy is such wasted and negative energy.**

There is nothing good that could come from that. It's something that I've been working on for the past few years and someone said to me once, "Jealousy works in the opposite way that you want it to."

And it's so true, when you see a guy with something you want, and you think, "Oh fuck, I wish I had that. Why does he deserve it?" That doesn't bring what you want closer to you, it actually pushes it further away. Whereas if you see someone that has something you admire or a trait that you possess and you think to yourself, "Oh man, bless that guy, he's worked hard for that. That's his good luck that he's got that," and you send out positive energy toward him, I feel like it's far more likely that you'll have the thing that is it you're looking for.

Mike:

Obviously people are jealous of the outcomes, but they don't see the struggle. A good example of that, is my roommate and really close friend is a very, very successful lawyer. And I lived with him and a lot of people say, "Why are you putting so much time into *Danger & Play* instead of putting time into being this hardcore lawyer that you once were?" And I said, "Well, because I saw what my friend goes through."

Yes, he has amazing financial rewards, but to be a really successful lawyer is a grind. I'm sure people see this guy and think, "Oh, I'm so jealous, how come his wife looks like this or how come his car looks like that or his house is so big?" Well, why don't you live with that guy for a couple weeks, and then you can tell me if you're still jealous.

Nic G:

Yeah.

Everything has its price and I guess the question is, are you prepared to pay it?

And financial success is a huge one of those. There are certain individuals... I just really started to take my business seriously over the last few years and sure, I don't have the money problems I used to have, but fuck man, I work for that money way harder than I ever have before. And sometimes I have to ask myself, "Is this trade off of my time and life energy worth the financial remuneration?" And sometimes I actually think the answer is no. In general, I think it's yes, but sometimes I think the answer is no.

Mike:

Yeah, a friend of was kind of teasing me but I was complaining: I said, "Man, my hosting bill is going to be so high because my traffic has been blowing up," and he said, "Oh, humble-brag," and I said, "Man, that's not a humble brag, it sucks." You build this successful website and you think "Yeah, my site's growing, isn't this amazing?" And then all of a sudden, your site is crashing and you have to upgrade to a different server, and then you have another problem and you can't keep up with emails people send you. You really do trade in one problem for another set of problems.

Nic G:

Yeah, to an extent. There were two things I wanted to say on that. The first that I'd rather be wealthy and have problems than poor and have problems. I know it's a clichéd statement, but a friend of mine was in an exchange program, he lived in the States during high school. He's from France originally, but he lived with a wealthy family in Aspen and he was having a chat with the father of the family and the guy said to him:

"John, you don't understand, but with success and wealth come a whole new set of problems and you have no idea what they are until you reach those levels of wealth and success."

And that was something that really, really made me think.

Mike:

So what's your philosophy on money or what is enough? Because for me generally, I have an idea of what is enough, and it isn't that big number that these Wall Street guys would give you.

You know they call it, what's your "Fuck You" number? When you have that amount that you don't want to do anything. And I've learned that really the only thing that I value out of money is that I don't have to put up with as much bullshit to make money.

Nic G:

Yeah, that's an interesting perspective. It's a subject I spend a great deal of my time thinking about. So the first thing I'll say is... an example, I used to work with someone who was quite a wealthy individual. He made his money in the stock market and he didn't ever have to work again. And I realized that he was no happier than I was. And at this point I was struggling financially, a struggling jiu-jitsu teacher, I wasn't making much money and I realized that he was no happier than I was. A lot unhappier in many ways. He had this sound system. I mean I'm a HUGE music lover, it's one of the best things in my life, my music and listening to music.

And he had this stereo system worth $100,000, maybe $150,000. Super high-end stereo system. And he never listened to it. It just sat in his apartment and he never listened to it. If he did listen to it, he kept the volume on real low. And I realized... I had bought a $150 pair of headphones that I had researched on the Internet and spent a lot of time looking into and I used those every day for like six hours a day, and I realized that I had gotten so much more out of them that he did than this ridiculously expensive sound system.

And I see that that's a common theme with wealth because everything is relative.

Like you want to become wealthy and you want to drive a Lamborghini and you achieve those things and you get your Lamborghini and you take it for a drive and it's really fun for the first month and then it's like, "Hmmm, I'm kind of bored of this." You have to chase a bigger and bigger prize and I think that's the...

For me, it's having enough money to do a few things really well, like take a few decent vacations. It's not about stuff. For me, money has never been about buying things, it's been about freedom. That's why my number one value in life is freedom. And I'm always looking forward to the freedom that money can buy. I mean freedom from having to work and freedom from things that I don't want to do. So I think that ultimately that's what it comes down to for me, is freedom.

Mike:

Right. I did a whole podcast on finding your values and what you value the most, and freedom is one that I rate too. I put it sort of, people say this is sort of childish, and I say well, okay. It is what it is. I just don't want to do what it is I don't want to do. And it sounds so simplistic and I still manage to accomplish quite a bit of stuff, so it isn't like I don't want to do anything, but when you have enough money that you can do what you want to do, then you're fine.

Now I guess for everybody, that number's going to vary. My needs are simple. I don't need a Lamborghini or Ferrari, I rent my apartment, and I don't need a multi-million dollar mansion. And I notice that the people who buy those things, they actually lose freedom because those things start to own them.

They have a mortgage, then they have to worry about scratching the car. They can't even enjoy the car because they're afraid to leave it outside because somebody might scratch it. They are paranoid that the valet is in there trying to steal and they become obsessed with these material possessions.

Nic G:

Yeah, so you paraphrased one of my favorite movie quotes ever which is from *Fight Club:* sooner or later the things you own start to own you.

As an example, just over the last year, I don't have an apartment, I have hardly any material possessions. I have two suitcases worth of possessions and I've never been happier. It's such a freeing thing. I mean, sometimes I'll go teach a jiu-jitsu seminar somewhere and someone will want to give me a t-shirt to thank me for coming there, and I always have to politely decline because I just look at that t-shirt for what it is. It's extra baggage for me, and on a micro-level, a loss of freedom.

And the world... I think it's strange that um, I'm starting to realize that when you look for the truth or when you seek truth, you find that the truth is pretty much the exact opposite of what you were taught to believe. David DeAngelo calls it the critical counterintuitive.

He says that if you want to succeed in any sphere or field or endeavor, look at what everyone else is doing and do the exact opposite.

And if you look at what our society is saying to us is, buy more stuff. You know? Get more things. Even more. Achieve more.

And what I'm starting to realize from my own perspective is, actually, have less things. Maybe a few quality things, but have less things and free yourself from all of that. And that's what's making me happy. It just fascinates me that there's a bunch of different things that I don't know about. Things where, society has trained me in one way and I still believe those ways and ultimately critical counterintuitive and I'm always looking for those things and I love finding them.

Can you identify any of those in your life?

Mike:

I actually met a guy who lived kind of like you do now. He said, "My kids are out of college now, I'm divorced. I've had the Lamborghinis, the Ferraris, and Mansions." He's part of a subculture where you live out of a suitcase.

Your entire life can fit in a suitcase. So he had a foldable parker thing and he just travelled everywhere and I thought, "Wow, that's really cool." And the same thing happened to me, after I got divorced I went to stay with my friend and the plan was that I'll stay with him for a couple weeks, sleep on his futon, and then go find an apartment of my own.

I slept on a futon. All of my belongings fit in a suitcase. It was great. Because I felt like I could get up anywhere and do anything wherever I wanted instead of having obligations to things I don't really even care that much about.

I believe family obligations are important. Your friends are important. But obligations to, "What if somebody scratches my car?" You know, Joe Rogan had a good story where he said, "My car got dinged and I got really mad and was pissed off," and he thought, "Well, why do I care? It'll cost $500, I have $500. I can fix my car door, and here I am getting so angry and so enraged and so obsessed because I have a dent in my car, when that's the stupidest thing in the world that I should ever worry about."

Nic G:

Yeah. That's a cool story. That's what I'd expect from Joe. There's another thing I thought about which is:

Anything that can be taken away from you, is not you.

And a lot of people tie up their identity or self-worth in what they own or in their career. And the question I always ask myself is, "If this were to be taken away from me tomorrow, how would I feel?"

And with material possessions there are one or two things that would make me feel really shitty and that's because I really need them for work, like my computer or my jiu-jitsu gi, but besides all that, it's just bullshit man.

Mike:

OK, if something was taken away from you, what would you do? My question is, what if you could no longer do jiu-jitsu because some magician cast a spell that took jiu-jitsu out of your life. So jiu-jitsu's gone, now what?

Nic G:

I'd just focus more on yoga. I'm really getting into yoga now. And I'll still use the energy that I put into jiu-jitsu. In fact, it's already happening. A lot of the energy that I was directing at becoming better at jiu-jitsu has now been transferred to yoga. But if someone said to me that I couldn't go jiu-jitsu anymore, I'd pretty much do yoga full time.

Mike:

And then you could do what you're doing now which is really cool.

A lot of people talk about lifestyle and lifestyle design and it's such an amorphous concept, but I think Nick embodies what you want to go for, is, his passion, his life is jiu-jitsu and then that's also his business.

He sells gis, he has an association, and he does seminars. He has a really good book that I've read and going to link to. And he's able to design everything around what he does and even if you took away his jiu-jitsu, he could just do that with yoga.

Nic G:

Yeah, I probably could transfer that over into yoga or some other industry if I really wanted to. Again, I think the foundation, not for everyone, but for many people, if you want to look at the foundation of a business you want to start I guess the first question is:

Will being involved in that industry be fun for me and will I enjoy it?

And sure, you could probably make it work if the answer is no, but it'll be a lot easier and more fun if the answer's yes.

Mike:

Because a lot of people don't realize that there's a lot of un-fun stuff. For example, how many hairs have we pulled out of our heads talking about web design and stuff like that?

Nic G:

Yeah. Too many.

Mike:

And you're training for BJJ and everybody says, "Oh wow, he's a black belt," but what about the injuries? What about the pain?

Nic G:

Yeah dude, just the other day I was in Australia and I was teaching a seminar, which was great. I met a bunch of really cool people, but then this 20-year old purple belt kid was fucking almost beating me up you know? And I was like, "Fuck, how much longer can I keep doing this?" But it's just the cost, dude.

Everything comes with its cost. And again, you have to ask yourself the question: am I willing to pay the price?

Mike:

And jealousy comes from looking at what you have, and not what you went through to get it.

Nic G:

Yeah, you know that Buddhist expression, "Contentment is the one true wealth?" Oh, so you were talking about jealousy from another person's perspective, yeah. It's true. It's very true. In most cases, I would say that some people are just born with a certain gift or talent that they didn't have to work too hard for, but they are the freak exceptions, not the rule.

Mike:

Yeah, they are definitely the exception. There are a few people with that prodigy talent. But what happens to them is they often burn out because they never had to work for it.

An example is, he still worked for it, let's take somebody like Kevin Randleman, he was a NCAA D1 all-star wrestler, but because he had such gifts, his MMA career was nothing like it should have been.

If you want to, Rampage [Jackson] is another guy, talk about a guy with amazing genetics for fighting and although they did well, they're not at the pinnacle that they would have been if they'd had the work ethic of someone like Fedor who doesn't have a natural fighter's physique.

Nic G:

Yeah. My favorite example is GSP [George St-Pierre]. Because he is someone who had genetic potential, but he didn't just rest on that, he worked his ass off, you know?

There's that expression, "Hard work beats talent every time," but I'll tell you straight up, hard work plus talent beats anything else. So I think one of the important things to do is to look at look at your natural skillset or your natural talent and abilities. Then decide if you'd be willing to work hard on them, then look at the nexus point of where those two meet. And that's how you can do well at business or anything else in life.

Mike:

Had you tried anything before BJJ that you failed at?

Nic G:

Umm, not really man. I went to college and stuff and I was training jiu-jitsu already, I guess you could say I failed in business. Well, not failed, but didn't make a huge success of a couple of businesses that I'd started in my late teens, early 20s. And I put them on the back burner to focus on jiu-jitsu, so now it's come full circle.

Now I'm focusing on business again. So yes and no, I guess.

Mike:

That brings me to one of our questions which is, if you had to go back 10 years, what is one thing that you wish you had learned?

Nic G:

That's a great question and the answer for me at this point is... I've been watching this show called Oprah's master class. I noticed a theme: she interviews all these successful and actualized people and, she asks a similar question, and one of the themes that keep recurring is, just listen to that own inner voice and to trust your instincts.

When I was younger, I wish I had just followed my instincts more, not so impressionable and swayed by popular opinion and people around me, and to be honest I think I was far less impressionable and easily swayed than the average person, but if I had blocked it all out entirely, there's no telling how far ahead I'd be today.

Mike:

What was your instinct that you weren't listening to?

Nic G:

Specifically in regards to jiu-jitsu, the answer I think of is, I kept thinking that I had to be the best competitor ever to actualize myself as a jiu-jitsu practitioner. My body was getting beat up all the time and I was tired, I didn't feel good and I just kept pushing on and pushing on and my instinct was telling me that "there has to be a better way than this."

That there has to be a way to align health and feeling good with jiu-jitsu. And it was only when I took my eye off those competitor prizes that I was able to say, "Okay, cool, now I should listen to this voice that's been bugging me for this long time and focus on my health. Start doing yoga and things like that."

Mike:

Yeah. It's interesting that we often ignore what our inner voice or whatever we want to call it, is telling us. For example, I always kind of liked nerdier people and I wish that I had hung out with nerdier people in high school and college rather than thinking, "Who's cool and who's not?" Because when you get older, you realize that the so-called "cool people" are nothing but trend followers. And they don't really have anything going on in five or ten years and the people who are the nerds are actually the ones who have shit going on.

Nic G:

It's not easy to hear that voice because you haven't learned how to hear it.

You are so used to sitting down and playing video games for four hours a day, which I was. Or you are so distracted by mass media and all the things you have going on in your life that you just can't hear that voice. One of the guests on *The Journey*, he said, "The mind speaks very loudly, but the heart speaks very softly." And that stuck with me and I realized that things like meditation are what allow you to hear that voice. And until you can hear it, there is no point in trying to follow it because you'll be distracted, you'll be hearing the wrong things.

Mike:

Right. People will ask me, "Well, how do I find my life's purpose or how do I find out what I want to do with my life?" And I say, "Turn off all your televisions and your gadgets and just go sit in a room all by yourself with your thoughts, and that terrifies people. But that's how you find yourself.

Nic G:

And you'll tell them that, and none of them will do it, they want you to give them an easy answer. They want you to say is, "All you need to do is read this book and you'll be fine. Or all you need to do is go to this website and it will give you the answer."

Very few want to sit and face themselves and look for the answer to these questions in the hard way, which is being frustrated while meditating and not noticing results. Being disciplined. No one wants to do that.

Mike:

Right. And they find out, the deeper you go, the deeper the hole is. That's when the panic comes in. You've rejected all of the values that people have given you. Now you are rudderless and you feel like you have been cast asunder and that's very painful and anxious, but that's your journey. Everybody's journey is individual. That's why I like the name of your podcast, *The Journey*.

Everybody, whether they know it or not, is on a journey. Some people are being guided like sheep by shepherds on their journey. Other people sort of think, "Why am I with these people going on that? Why don't I go on my own journey?"

And ultimately that's what we have to do: we have to find our own journey.

Nic G:

Yeah, like I mentioned earlier, it's just remarkable how many hugely successful, actualized people say that exact thing. "It's like I had this inner drive or this inner voice that just kept pointing me in this direction or pulling me in this direction or it kept telling me to do something."

That is the reward for listening to that voice, because when you listen to it, it's not easy, dude. The rest of the world is going to say you're crazy. I was teaching jiu-jitsu in London, I had a reasonably good gig there and then I just decided to leave and just go teach jiu-jitsu seminars around the world and I don't have a fixed address.

And a lot of people are like, "What are you doing? Why are you doing this?" It made them uncomfortable. And fortunately, I had the courage to stick with it and it seems to have worked out.

Mike:

Right. And then we got to remember the Zen parable or Zen rule where a guy, his son falls off a horse and breaks his arm and people say, "Isn't that terrible, your son broke his arm?" And the father says, "We'll see." And then the army comes to recruit people and they didn't take his son because his son had a broken arm and they say, "Well, isn't that great?" And he said, "We'll see."

And really, that is the journey: "We'll see." It really isn't over 'til it's over. What you think is a catastrophe now might not be such a catastrophe. The things that you view now, well they might be good or it all could change tomorrow.

All you have to do is recognize that you are on a journey and just embrace it.

Nic G:

Yeah. The point I'd like to be at one day which I know I'm nowhere fucking near is to just have detachment from all outcomes. And it's my understanding that enlightened Zen masters don't really perceive, label or judge anything as good or bad. They just accept everything as it is.

And that's something that, to a large extent, something that meditation has helped me with. And I hope it takes me to that point because there are still times in my life where something will happen like you say, there will be a metaphorical arm break in my life and I'm like, "Ahh fuck," and as you said, it will turn out to be not what I expected. And I'd like to get to the point where I would like to supersede all of that.

Mike:

Right. Turning off that judge is so hard. There was a parable that I posted on the site once and it really made a bunch of guys mad. And I asked them, "Why'd it make you mad?"

And the parable was something like this. A Zen master is being chased by a tiger, and he got to edge of a cliff, fell off and was then holding on for dear life and then he noticed a flower, the petals of the flower and how it was white and the beauty of the flower and that was the end of the story.

People were like, "How could he just look at the flower? He's about to die. Man up and be alpha and try to save himself." And you realize it's just a different level of consciousness where you are living in the moment and not worried about the outcome "if I fall down and smash my head."

"Here I am, I'm in the moment, isn't this flower beautiful?"

Nic G:

Yeah. There's something a friend of mine told me a few months ago which is the fact that, we were speaking about gratitude and I was saying how I've got this gratitude journal and I give thanks to things every day and, he said, "Yeah I've been doing the same thing and not only do I give thanks to everything that I have, but I've been giving thanks for everything I don't have."

And it made me realize that a lot of people society looks at as having things that they want, are very, very miserable. And one of the examples I always think of is Britney Spears. She's got all the money and fame she could possibly want and it hasn't made her happier. Many people would argue it's made her feel horrible.

And you'll see kids in favelas in Brazil who have nothing but an old paint can to kick around as a football and they have the biggest smiles on their face. So again, it comes back to, the things that you were taught that will make you happy aren't necessarily the things that will make you happy.

Mike:

A lot of times, it's a lack of spiritual grounding too, I think. I think that because we no longer believe in God that people have taken that a little bit too far and they say, "There is no god, no Judeo-Christian god, therefore there is no spiritual element." In a way, we are spiritually bankrupt.

Nic G:

Yeah. The way I look at that is, my favorite spiritual teacher Osho, he says:

"There is no god, but I've found something superior which is godliness."

And that's the recognition that everything is divine. Everything. Whether it's the fucking dog turd on the street that you walked by or a flower or whatever it is that we experience in reality, it's a divine aspect of God and part of creation.

And I think that's a much healthier way. I don't even know if that's true, it's just what I feel is true, but either way I think it's much healthier to look at the world like that than to think of some angry man in the sky watching everything that you're doing or the alternative that this is a freak accident and we are these reductionist mechanistic that is just consuming resources in a mad scramble for survival.

Mike:

Right. [Criticizing the view point of] we're bacteria in a Petri dish and that's all there to life. And when you think that way, all you do is chase material pleasure because you have eliminated the spiritual component of your life. "There is no spirit, there is no unconscious. That's all garbage. If I can't observe it, it doesn't exist."

Well, what can I observe? I can observe material sensations, I can observe sex. A new car. A bigger house. And then, that's all that you chase. You have material wealth but spiritual bankruptcy. And that's why a lot of people who are rich, I always say, "It's easy to say this when you're rich." But then they realize after getting rich that money doesn't matter.

Now, of course, money matters, because if you can't pay your bills, it's stressful etc. But they realize there is more to reality and more to your existence than material possessions and material sensations.

Nic G:

Yeah. And again, I'm not against material possessions and material sensations. In fact, I'm all for them, I just think ultimately these two things—being rich in spirit and rich in material possessions—aren't necessarily mutually exclusive. Or diametrically opposed.

And with my life, that's my mission, I want to have everything I want or need on the material plane and also be grounded on the spiritual plane. I don't think there's a need to separate them and one doesn't preclude the other.

Mike:

Do you think that ayahuasca has put you more in touch with the spiritual plane?

Nic G:

So funny you ask that, because I was just having this discussion with someone yesterday. And the best way I can describe it is that before ayahuasca, I was a very mechanical person. Very reductionist and business-like in all my decisions and view of the world. And the way it feels after doing a bunch of ayahuasca is that I've become more of an organic entity.

Everything has a "softer edge" to it. I know that's not a very good way to explain it, but that's pretty much the only way I can.

Mike:

It put you in touch with your vulnerabilities, didn't it?

Nic G:

I guess so. Sure as hell exposed them. So yeah, I have to say yes to that.

Mike:

One thing I've noticed about alpha-type guys or high-achiever guys is that they tend to live in denial of their vulnerabilities. That means they only focus on what they are strong about and they ignore anything that might be an insecurity, because they view that as weakness instead of accepting that as part of themselves. And when you use a compound like DMT or ayahuasca, or in my case, I used 5-MeO-DMT, you start to realize that you have a lot less control than you think you have.

There is a lot more going on than you think is going on. Control... I don't know if I would say the control is completely illusory, I may reach that conclusion in one point in my life, but control is definitely overstated and we have far less control than we think.

And because of that, I've been more comfortable with my own vulnerability.

Nic G:

Yeah. There's an expression from the book *Peaceful Warrior*, in which this mentor said to his student, "Being a warrior isn't about invulnerability, it's about absolute vulnerability." And I think there is a tendency for, as you say, the alpha-types, men who are going out there in the world to make their mark and achieve and succeed, if you think about it, they almost become soldier-like or they embody a lot of characteristics of a soldier.

If you think about a soldier on a battlefield, he's armored, right? He has protection on. Because he has to be, because he's under attack always. And I can understand why men, myself included, build up that rigidness and that armor and the problem is, that keeps you closed off from a lot of things.

I'm not saying it needs to be removed entirely, but you need to know where the armor is too thick or not thick enough

Mike:

It makes you a far better writer and better able to connect. Somebody asked me recently, "Why did you start deciding to expose yourself?" In terms of anything that's happened to me, I have no problem putting it online. I used to fear judgment. I used to have shame, "What if I reveal that component of myself?"

And then I got to the point where I said, "When I write something, I want to feel like I want to delete what I wrot,e because I put myself out there and I made myself too vulnerable." And then I thought, "Well, why are you afraid of being vulnerable?" Because really, it was a fear. It was a fear that I had to conquer.

Nic G:

·Yeah.

So there's this theory that every fear has its roots ultimately in the fear of death. And that's what people don't like about vulnerability. It's the fear of their own mortality.

Something that I've meditated on a lot is that I'm going to die one day. And there might not be anything after that. Once I internalized that and accepted that, I found that it was a lot easier to just to say to people, "This is who I am."

And you spoke a lot about it earlier, we had a long conversation about it, I took a lot of insight from you on the concept of haters. I asked you, "How do I deal with haters?" And you said to me, the people who usually hate on you are usually bottom-feeders. They are not the ones whose opinions matter anyway. I guess no one's opinions really matter.

Something I read the other day, "I used to worry about other people's opinions until I tried to pay my bills using them." And that stuck with me a lot.

I realized it's not my responsibility what other people think of me, it's only my responsibility of what I think of myself.

Mike:

And part of the journey is finding yourself, being whole, and self-actualized and self-possessed. When you mention the fear of death, that's funny, because if you think about the metaphors we use in our everyday language. Well, think about this one: "You're sticking your neck out." You are exposing your neck. You are making yourself vulnerable. Even though you are only doing it by revealing a part of your personality that might be weak, or maybe by using something in your past that somebody might try to use against you. What you are doing is you're holding your neck, and that goes into our primal roots where somebody can bite your neck and kill you.

So part of the quest then is you overcome those fears. If you are afraid of being vulnerable and afraid of expressing who you are, you are missing out on a major part of what it means to be a man, and I mean that sincerely. I think that little boys are afraid of vulnerability and as you transition from a little boy to a man, you recognize with wisdom that you have vulnerabilities and you accept those.

Nic G:

Yeah, but again, you can very easily swing too far to the other end of the spectrum. No one likes the dudes who start crying at the sappiest scene in a movie or at the drop of a hat, or his girlfriend looks at him wrong and he's like, "I just feel so vulnerable right now."

I mean, no one wants that. That's an aspect of being a man, sometimes you have to fucking be in a difficult situation and not show vulnerability. But you have a problem when you can't turn that off. When you are just a rigid badass permanently. And you cannot show any softness and you cannot expose yourself or that vulnerable side of yourself. That's when the problems happen.

Mike:

There's always going to be duality. And focusing on one and being completely vulnerable is masculine, but not focusing on it at all isn't going to be masculine. And I think that nowadays. men have a bigger problem with coming into terms with their own vulnerabilities and I don't mean. "Oh I watched a Hallmark movie or Lifetime movie that made me cry." But the idea that it's okay to be anxious because you haven't found your life's purpose. It's okay if you don't know what you want to do with your life.

It's okay if you don't know what you're going to do in five years. The idea that, "You're 18, what's your major? What do you do when you graduate college?" It's okay to not know and just say, "I don't know."

Now, on the other hand it's not okay to be aimless and never have a plan or even care. So part of being who you want to be is dealing with those different forces that are pulling you in different directions.

Nic G:

Yeah. I noticed a theme that ran throughout this whole conversation today, it's as you said, duality. And I've noticed more and more that it's almost like a life art or life skill.

One of the most important life arts or life skills is to be able to walk that line in every aspect of your life. That line between being vulnerable and not too vulnerable.

Or making money and making too much money.

I can think of loads of examples from this chat, but it's an art.

Mike:

Well, give me some examples.

Nic G:

Jiu-jitsu is one. There is a fine line between training too much and training enough. And you can very easily fall over into the overtraining spectrum of things, and then you get injured and tired and burned out. Or if you don't train enough you don't progress, and it's your job to use your intelligence and feedback loops that your body and mind provide to decide, "How much do I need to train?"

It's no one else's responsibility, it's yours. It's your responsibility if you're the lawyer who's making 60 grand per month but is totally burned out and feeling like shit all the time to say to yourself, "Maybe I will be better off working 60 percent of the time and making only $30,000 per month." It's your responsibility. You got to walk the line.

And again, it comes back to one of my very favorite expressions of all time which is, "The destiny of the warrior is balance in all things."

And it's one of the things that I'm trying to live my life by at the moment.

Mike:

Right. The lawyer example is so funny because a lot of my friends are what I would call "victims of their own success." And I say, well, why are you working so hard, you could cut down our cases, you don't have to take that many cases. You don't have to make $900,000 this year or $1.5 million this year. Why don't you just make $250,000? Are you really that much happier than you would be otherwise? And they don't stop and ask. They don't reflect, "Is this really getting me the outcomes that I want?"

Instead they keep chasing a dragon or chasing something that somebody else told them to chase, and what do they find? They find heartache, anxiety, misery, stress, and heart attacks.

Nic G:

Yeah. You're a perfect example. You're a qualified lawyer and what are you going today? It's Friday, you're sitting in the sun and we're recording a podcast. You're having fun, you're having a chat. How many of your contemporaries from law school are doing that right now? I mean. most of them are probably stressed to their fucking eyeballs. Had to have a 20 oz latte to get through the second half of the day. They are stressed, they won't be able to switch off properly tonight without getting blind drunk. And is the money really worth that?

And I don't know, that's a question only the individual can answer.

Mike:

Yeah. A question I like to ask is: what's the prize? If you are telling me that you want to win something, then I'm going to go into your frame then. I'm not going to tell you that your contest is the wrong contest to enter. What's the prize?

And most people can't answer it.

Well uhh, if that's the prize, is that really what you want?

And very few people actually stop and think, okay, I'm in this contest whether it's conscious or not and a lot of times it's unconscious. They are in an unconscious contest with everyone else without realizing it. And nobody stops and says, "Okay, if I win, what do I win? What's the prize?"

Nic G:

So I'm going to flip that back on you and ask you: what is the prize that you're chasing?

Mike:

Right now, I'm definitely not chasing a prize. And that's what's great. I don't feel like I'm in a contest with anyone and I feel like I'm living my purpose, living my calling, I'm contributing to others, so if there is a prize it's the fulfillment that I get from helping other people, because that's the stage in life where I'm at.

I'm not chasing things or possessions so I would say that I'm not really in a contest any more. And it feels very liberating to feel like when I wake up, I'm not running a rat race against a hundred other rats. I'm sure I'm running my own race in my own ways but I would say more like I'm climbing the mountain rather than running a race.

Nic G:

Well, there's no way I can improve on that answer. That sounds pretty good.

Mike:

We're not doing too bad for an impromptu coffee shop discussion. So we do want to get in a few reader questions. The first one is a fun one and somebody asked you a variation of this on your Reddit AMA which is:

"When did you realize that there is nothing waiting for you in the future that is any better than what is waiting for you right now?"

Nic G:

It wasn't a lightning bolt realization, it didn't just happen all at once. It's something that over time, gradually became clear to me, just through introspection.

And the way I did that was that I noticed that every time I got something I wanted or had been desiring, the enjoyment or pleasure or feeling of sense of achievement that I had derived from that lasted only a short while before it was replaced with another desire.

And the best example I can think of is, a couple years back there was this girl I thought that was so fucking attractive, and I thought, "I've always wanted a girl like that." I got together with her, and after a while I started getting bored of her and I just wasn't fulfilled any more. The same thing happened when I got a black belt in jiu-jitsu. It was an amazing feeling and something I had been working toward my whole life, and then after a while it just wore off and became... I took it for granted, almost.

I realized that there's got to be a better way. There's got to be a smarter way to approach life and to be constantly chasing micro-rewards or macro-rewards, that I think is the goal of Buddhism and the goal of enlightenment: to just be happy constantly or be happy with whatever you have. Irrespective of the circumstances and the outcomes and to be desireless. And it's nowhere near where I'm at, but I am moving closer towards that. As the more I move towards that, the happier I become.

Mike:

Yeah, it's an amazing accomplishment to have a BJJ black belt and it's funny that you said, you were probably like, "Yeah, this is really cool." But you wake up the next day, you still have your life to live.

People think, "What happens when I make that first million dollars, right?" One year I made a million dollars. After taxes, it was less. And what did I say?

"Wow, this is cool." Okay. You wake up the next day though, and that's your life. Life goes on. It isn't like one event happens that's going to totally alter the course of your life where if you win one prize, suddenly your life is different. You can sit with me, I'm just bumming around in bum clothes, I don't care. I don't look like a man of means or whatever. Because what? Your life is what it is. You still have the same problems. You are still on the same journey.

So people would say, "Nick, you got the first BJJ black belt from Roger Gracie," and it's a worthy goal, but ultimately, you've got to find something else.

Nic G:

Yeah, I think a Zen master or a Buddhist master would be as happy sitting down drinking his latte or his green tea or whatever it is as he would be to hear the news that he'd made a million dollars or was awarded a black belt or whatever.

To hear the news of a friend's death. He would have just gone beyond that emotional pendulum that we find ourselves swinging from. And again, it's not something I have claimed to achieved, but it is something that I'm definitely hoping to one day.

Mike:

There's a certain irony to it too, and it's very hard to for all of us with our classical Western minds and our logical minds to understand, and people will think, "Well, you talk about this Zen stuff and living in the moment, but only losers live in the moment and don't chase goals."

But you know, you've had some success in life, I've had some success in life and it's really bizarre that you can live in the moment and you can still achieve your goals. The difference is that they are your goals, and it's what you want to do and it's how you find fulfilment. And that's the difference I think. I think it's how you can reconcile these Eastern concepts with the Western mind is:

Living in the moment doesn't mean you walk around aimlessly, living in the moment makes you mindful of what you are doing. But when you are mindful of what you are doing, what happens? You start to achieve mastery.

Nic G:

Yeah, and again, let's take it back to the idea of balance.

I don't think it's very easy to live an enlightened and enjoyable life if you've got nothing and you're just walking the streets as a tramp and you have no dignity in your life, but for me, everything that I'm working towards is ultimately to facilitate me to be able to live in the moment more.

So the reason that I want financial freedom is that I can practice yoga more and meditate more and not be stressed out by work. It's not to have money to buy things. For me, that is the main difference: the goals and everything that I'm working towards and my desires are all ultimately leading me back to a point where finding myself in the present moment is an easier ideal to obtain.

Mike:

You can find yourself in the present moment in the task of making money. That's something too that people don't think of. I enjoy the hell out of my websites and I don't really make a living off of them, but I'm making some money off of them. And I'm finding enjoyment in the things that I do with the website and you are making a lot of your money online, you live in the moment and you enjoy it don't you?

Nic G:

Yeah. It's true. And also, there's this guy I referenced earlier in the podcast, named David DeAngelo, also known as Eben Pagan, and something that always stuck with me that he said was that the more he focuses on the future, the better his life becomes now.

I remember when I was in Australia a couple months back and I was teaching a seminar and I was rolling, doing jiu-jitsu. At the end of the class, we were all sparring and I put on this really cool music and I was just really in the moment and I was so happy I was almost overcome with emotion, and I realized that that moment was only able to be created by all the effort that I had put in and all the goals that I had put in place.

So again, it's that balance in life. Finding the balance between being in the moment and being able to plan for the future.

Mike:

Do you have any exercises to get into the moment? I'll tell you what I do a lot of the time. When I feel like I'm getting anxious or being bothered by something, I just stop and I meditate actively on what I'm doing. "Okay, I'm sitting in a chair and wearing grey pants and there's my phone. There's a microphone in front of me. It's white and it has these sort of black ribbons and the red light is on and it says B-L-U-E," and I find that once I become consciously aware of what I'm doing, then all that self-talk kind of goes away and I find myself kind of in the moment.

Do you have an exercise that you do that helps you get into the moment?

Nic G:

Yeah, meditating at night before I go to sleep. Doing a proper 30-minute or 40-minute meditation helps me feel more in the moment the next day. For some reason, I wake up the next day and I'm much more in the moment. But also, an on-the-spot technique that I use is a combination of two things:

1. Just taking a deep breath. Literally deep, like [demonstrates]. And focusing on the breath and the feel of the breath. The sound of the breath.

In addition to that, I call it externalization. Because the problem with a lot of the nature of the work that we all do, it's very abstract and it pushes you into your head. Like when you read. For example, we're all sitting in front of the computer reading, most of us are doing that as part of our job. And what this is doing is causing a very mental sort of state. And I don't mean mental like psychopathic, I just mean you are in your mind.

2) Externalization: so when you externalize and start focusing on things around you. As you said, looking at the microphone, right? For me, I look up, I look at the sun. I look off into the distance. I get a feel for the sun on my skin. I look at all these external things that are going on and that helps bring me into the moment.

Mike:

Those are great exercises that we unfortunately don't learn. And that's another thing that I wish I had learned ten years ago. What do you wish you had learned ten years ago? Well, how to make a living on the Internet. That would have been where I spent a lot of time, because now I'm playing catch-up and number two, how to get into the moment, because when you are in the moment, anxiety just goes away. Anxiety is an obsession with uncertain future outcomes.

That's all anxiety is. "You're not good enough. Is this girl going to turn me down if I approach her or am I not going to be able to pay my rent this month? What's going to happen?"

But the future is always uncertain, so I wish that I'd have known there's an exercise you can do that could get you into the moment. Could you imagine if you had known this stuff when you were like fourteen years old?

Nic G:

Ahh, dude! A friend of mine was telling me recently that she started meditating when she was seven. Her mom was big into meditation. They lived on a ranch, they had a bunch of employees, and at the end of each day she required that everyone sat in a circle and meditate for 20 minutes or whatever it was.

And I just thought to myself, that there's no telling... although that's probably not a good way to think about it, I mean my life might have taken a very negative turn if I had been meditating my whole life. Things are exactly as they should be.

Mike:

Right. You change one aspect of your life today, everything could change. You change one aspect of your life in ten years and everything would change, but the interesting thing is that it's such a framing issue, because if you had meditated when you were seven, you'd be at a different place in your life and you'd be just as happy as you are now. But it would have been a completely different road.

You might actually be in a monastery in Tibet, you know? Who knows? Or you might have been trying to climb Mount Everest. You might have been on Wall Street. Who knows where your life would have been?

But it definitely would have changed. That's one thing that you guys can take away from the podcast: the value of living in the moment. It would be, don't dismiss all these Eastern concepts as being weak-minded or weak-willed or showing that you lack purpose. And open yourself up to the possibilities that being so psychotic and focused and goal-driven all the time actually isn't the best way to go.

Nic G:

Oh man, I agree wholeheartedly. It's been my experience that it doesn't lead to happiness and actually moves you away from it.

Mike:

Well thanks a lot for being on the show. Of course I have to remind you guys, he has a great book, *The Blackbelt Blueprint*, and I will link to it at the end of the post. Thanks again for coming onto the show.

Nic G:

Thank you so much my friend, and keep up the good work with *Danger & Play*. I've actually been really enjoying your posts. Also, if you guys want to check out my podcast, you can find it at, www.TheJourneyPodcast.com.

Mike:

And I will link to his podcast and the blog at the bottom of the post. Thanks again for tuning in, and until next time, this is Mike from DangerAndPlay.com.

Disobey Fear

There's a feeling that arises in the pit of your stomach. Maybe the bosslady came into the office and is looking over your shoulder. You're lectured about TSP reports. Maybe some teacher calls you into his office. Maybe you step into the gym, fearful that you don't belong because you are fat, weak.

Whatever the situation, we all understand that feeling. It's an unconscious feeling. Your stomach tightens and your body language closes off.

Most people submit. You have been taught to submit.

The fear sets in and you… obey.

You should listen to that fear. Then you should disobey it.

That feeling tells you it might be time to commit murder: to kill the *old* you.

Fear is telling you to hold on to whatever identify or life you've created. Fear wants you to hold on. Fear despises growth and change.

The weak sloppy you that you're afraid of looking at in the mirror? I've been there. Fear told me to stay home. Won't people laugh at a fat guy in the gym?

I disobeyed the fear.

I used to be fat; no, *obese*. Now people trying making fun of me for being "too alpha."

The fear that would have kept me out of the gym would have kept the old me alive.

The old me is dead.

Disobey the fear. Kill the old you.

Why are you afraid of getting "caught" at work when you hate your job? Are you really going to starve? That's fear talking. You may lose your job or your friends or everything.

You will start over stronger.

Why are you holding on so tight to a life that is not yours? Why do you fear losing the approval of people you do not respect?

Fear is telling you to conform to a diseased, debased society.

Modern culture is controlled by fear-mongers, the debased, and the easily offended.

You must tip-toe around at work or at dinner parties, lest you offend someone.

Double standards abound. Mainstream media outlets mock domestic violence against men and tell you to pay that alimony and child support, because male privilege.

Why do you care if people you don't even like look at you funny? Why do you care if people hate you?

Fear is telling you to hold onto that you: *the old you.*

I haven't felt anything remotely resembling fear in a long time.

Yet the feeling surfaces, as it's deep within our unconscious.

As many know, I would often use Twitter as a way to counter-attack Gawker Media's message.

When you do that, nuance goes out the window, context is removed.

The social justice warriors are coming at me. The mainstream media is coming after me.

People are saying mean things on the Internet.

Why do I care?

I do care. I love it!

Does this mean I will no longer be welcome in respected society?

I won't be able to get a job at a large corporation with a huge HR department?

People who are vanilla and boring won't like me?

People who submit to SJWs as masters will never talk to me again?

The attacks are a blessing. The attacks remind me of my life's purpose and give me the opportunity to experiences a full-frontal attack by the media.

I welcome the hate. I love the attention. It makes me grow stronger.

The last bit of mainstream respectability I have is now dead.

At first, there was unconscious, irrational trepidation at the assaults. This made no sense to me. Why do I care?

Fear is unconscious. It tries taking control over you, to preserve your old life at all costs.

Talk yourself through the fear.

When the fear sets it, listen to it. Talk to it.

What is the fear telling you? The fear is telling you to hold on to a lifestyle you do not want to keep living.

The fear might be telling you it time to die: which means you will finally get to live.

It's time to live in a new home, a place of true freedom.

Test Yourself to Find Yourself

We live in odd and contradictory times. On one hand, every man believes he is an original. A unique snowflake. Special.

I see the Snowflake Complex in my email inbox every day. "I know you wrote this, Mike, but what about *me* and *my* situation?"

Yet those same "originals" regularly copy and rip off blog content from me and others.

If you are so original, why are you copying everyone else? Why do you act like everyone else? How can you live an original life?

There's a way to become an original. It's not what you'll hear about in a self-help book.

Stop finding yourself. Start testing yourself.

Navel-gazing (or *Omphaloskepsis*) may have had noble roots. One can learn much about himself and the world through living an examined life. Yet navel-gazing has taken on a new meaning in a culture of narcissism.

If you want to find yourself, what are you supposed to do?

Take a few personality quizzes, sit around, stare inside at your stupid emotions or talk about your mommy and daddy. Magically some insight is bound to occur.

Yet that hasn't worked for you, has it? When has sitting around emoting like a teenage schoolgirl or bored housewife ever helped you divine insights into yourself?

Trying to "find yourself" is something bored housewives in Lululemon pants do. They perform some stretches, read *Eat, Pray, Love,* and go around saying "namaste."

Where did this "find yourself" crap come from?

We live in a weak, self-indulgent, undisciplined society. In a society where weakness is elevated as a virtue, no one cares what you do. *Doing* is hard. *Imagining* and *speaking* (the cheapest of currencies) are valued above all else.

Do you doubt me? Live a decent life. Be a good parent. Donate to charity. Feed the poor. Volunteer in your community.

Make one offensive Tweet and see if anyone cares how you have actually lived your life. Likewise, you can live a deplorable life, abusing and cheating people, if you only say the right things.

As we are always a product of our culture, this weakness embedded itself in our unconscious minds. We've been brainwashed into believing that insight comes from what passes as thinking, rather than through challenging yourself.

Hence why we spend too much time thinking and emoting like hipsters rather than taking action like men.

Test yourself to find yourself.

Who are you? How are you different? There are many ways to find out. You may not like what you discover, which is one reason thinking (where you can imagine yourself as some hero) is elevated over doing (where reality sets in).

You think you're tough? Go to the gym. Hit it hard. If you're too sore to return, you're a pussy.

You think you're a ladies man? Go talk to some women. Find a woman who is so attractive that other people look at wonder what she is doing with you. Until then, you're a woman who reads too many *Twilight* and *50 Shades of Grey* novels.

Discover who you really are.

Right now. you're a copycat. You don't know who you are. And that's okay.

Everyone starts off as a brainwashed conformist. The system has spent a lot of time ensuring that you're a good little boy who doesn't cause any trouble.

There is no shame in being pathetic. There is great shame in refusing to find out who you really are.

"What if, on your last day, you met the man you could have become?"

Test yourself long enough and you will find yourself.

There are no short cuts. Self-help books and sites like *Danger & Play* can help you learn a trick or two.

But the other 90 percent is your responsibility.

How can you test yourself?

"Do something that scares you each day." – Unknown

The fear you feel is your unconscious mind reeling against a test. In school, you felt some sort of fear when a pop quiz happened, even if you knew the subject matter well.

I felt a rush of adrenaline when taking the California bar exam, even though intellectually I knew it'd be an easy test for me to pass. That fear of failure, of not being enough, always lurks. When you face your fears, you become someone new. The conformity slowly dies off. The brainwashed, sloppy, whiny, pathetic little lamb doesn't want to die.

What are you afraid of?

It doesn't matter to me. My fears are different from yours and my path differs from yours.

Find and face your fears and then you will become a true original.

About the Author

Mike Cernovich is a lawyer, author of "Gorilla Mindset," and host of the most successful mindset podcast on iTunes - The Mike Cernovich Podcast. His websites have been visited by millions of people.

Mike Cernovich's mindset techniques have helped countless improve their health and fitness, develop deeper personal and romantic relationships, and take control of anxiety and worry, and make more money.

As a child who grew up on welfare and was bullied, Cernovich had to build himself up from the ground up. He studied martial arts, boxed, became a California lawyer and published legal scholar, and most recently launched Gorilla Mindset, which is being labelled the how-to guide to life.

Cernovich knows everyone can live previously unimaginable by taking control of their health, fitness, nutrition, and mindset.

To learn more about how to improve your health and fitness and mindset, read:

Dangerandplay.com

Fit-juice.com

GorillaMindset.com

Cernovich also regularly updates a travel and marketing website:

Cernovich.com

You can also find him on:

272

Made in the USA
San Bernardino, CA
30 March 2017